Darrell Johnson

D

FACET **fb** BOOKS

BIBLICAL SERIES—19

John Reumann, General Editor

The Psalms

A Form-Critical Introduction

by HERMANN GUNKEL

with an Introduction
by James Muilenburg

translated by Thomas M. Horner

D0743571

FORTRESS PRESS   PHILADELPHIA

Translated from Volume I of the second edition of
Die Religion in Geschichte und Gegenwart
(Tübingen: J.C.B. Mohr [Paul Siebeck], 1930),
by arrangement with the publisher.

Library of Congress Catalog Card Number 67-22983

ISBN 0-8006-3043-2

Second Printing, 1969

Third Printing, 1972

3244A72   Printed in U.S.A.   1-3043

Introduction

U PON the roster of those who have contributed most significantly
and illuminatingly to our understanding of the records of the Old and
New Testaments, the name of Hermann Gunkel is inscribed indelibly
Were this *Who's Who* to be ordered according to importance of contribution or subsequent influence, there can be little doubt that he, like
Abou ben Adhem, would lead all the rest. His approach to the biblical
materials and his methodology in delineating their character and purpose have been appropriated, in one fashion or another, by all who
move in the mainstream of contemporary biblical studies. He gave new
direction to biblical scholarship, instilled vitality into research and rescued it from mere craftsmanship, opened fresh vistas for our grasp and
interpretation of the individual literary units, and, more than any other,
before or after, inspired in his students and successors an appreciation
of the true character of the many and diverse literary forms or genres
represented in the biblical records. No scholar excelled him in describ-
ing and illuminating the biblical modes of speech in all their nuances;
none equaled him in ability to transmit to his students the fascination
and excitement of biblical study.

In his early years as a student and then later as a professor at the
Universities of Halle (1889-94) and Berlin (1894-1907) Gunkel
came under the influence of some of the towering scholars of his day:
men like Heinrich Zimmern, the Orientalist; Paul de Lagarde, under
whom he studied Arabic; Eduard Meyer and Leopold von Ranke, the
historians; Adolf Erman, the Egyptologist; Paul Wendland and Eduard
Norden, the classical philologists; and Adolf von Harnack, the theolo-
gian and New Testament scholar. He was well-schooled in the methodol-

ogy of historical criticism, exemplified classically by Julius Wellhausen, notably in his monumental work *Prolegomena to the History of Ancient Israel* (1878). This approach sought to understand the books of the Bible by a critical analysis of their composition, their authorship, date, provenience, purpose, and sources.

While Gunkel recognized the validity of historical criticism as a legitimate, even necessary, discipline, he was convinced that it failed to answer many of the most natural and insistent questions raised not only by the modern reader, but by the biblical records themselves. He responded enthusiastically to the great work by J. G. Herder, *The Spirit of Hebrew Poetry* (1782-83), which followed the trail blazed by Bishop Richard Lowth's famous lectures at Oxford, *De sacra poesi Hebraeorum praelectiones academicae* (1753). In Herder he met one with a temper and cast of mind not unlike his own. Imagination and insight into the manners and nuances of speech, appreciation and literary sensitivity, openness to the whole world of Near Eastern culture as it found expression in the great literary monuments, and withal a rare ability to identify oneself in spirit and empathy with the mind and mood of the biblical writers in all their manifold ways of speaking, made it possible for him, as for Herder, to press scholarly inquiry beyond the confines of source analysis and phenomenological scrutiny. He knew how to *listen* to a text, and always insisted that it be read aloud in order that the reader might the better discern its movement and direction, its rhythm and assonance, its key words and accents. Research for him was as much an art as a science. He was insistent upon permitting the biblical speakers to have their say in their own fashion. He was aware they were *human* beings, like ourselves, and was not embarrassed in drawing upon contemporary history and everyday experience for the illumination of the ancient text. He recognized that in the pages of the Old and New Testament we have to do, not with literature in our modern understanding of *belles lettres*, but rather with extracts drawn from the daily life of persons and communities. This is not to say that he did not discern the aesthetic qualities of the biblical compositions; on the contrary he was rarely gifted in his ability to illuminate the many different genres of biblical speaking and the interior forces within the life of the people which gave them birth.

Gunkel was interested in writing a history of Israel's literature, and was convinced that historical criticism was insufficient for such a task. The isolation of the oldest traditions from their secondary accretions failed to penetrate the text itself, and did less than justice to the long period of oral transmission that often lay behind them. It was unable to provide any trustworthy chronological ordering of the materials since our knowledge of the dates of substantial sections of the Old Testament is too insecure. Moreover, large parts of the Old Testament are anonymous, and even where we do know the names of the writers, the biographical data are, with rare exceptions, almost completely wanting. What is more, Gunkel averred, the prevailing methodology of his time isolated Israel's literature and culture too completely from the wider environment of the other peoples of the ancient Near East, and consequently limited its horizons, obscured the function that the words were designed to serve, and failed to profit from the light that the cognate texts shed upon many biblical passages.

Since it is impossible, then, to write a history of Israel's literature in the conventional sense as a chronologically ordered and biographically oriented narrative, Gunkel proposed another way of viewing the materials, an approach that was at once more consonant with the Hebrew manner of speaking and more characteristic of Hebrew cultural mentality, where the typical and formal dominate over the individual and personal, especially in the earlier periods of Israel's history. The task of the literary historian is first of all to isolate the individual literary unit by determining its beginning and ending; he must then seek to identify its type or genre (*Gattung*) by observing its formal characteristics, style, mode of composition, terminology, and rhetorical features. Once the literary genre has been recognized and described, then its origin must be traced back to its provenience in the pre-literary stage of formulation. Since convention and custom determine to a considerable degree the fashioning and terminology of the literary types, Gunkel was intent upon collecting as many specimens or examples of each type as possible, not only within the Old Testament, but also in the related literary remains of the other peoples of the ancient Near East and even in Western culture. He perceived that much of the "literature" of the Old Testament was originally spoken, that its provenience was oral rather than written, and, like Martin Luther and Bishop Lowth and Herder, he sought to do justice to the speaking manner and oral style of each literary type and to release it from bondage to the printed page.

But the identification of the literary forms was only the first step in composing a literary history. One must inquire at one and the same time into the situation in personal or communal life in which the particular form or genre served its function, that is, the occasion in which this kind of speech was employed. Songs of victory were sung for the conquering hero upon his return from battle, dirges intoned over the bier of the dead, hymns chanted in the temple precincts, lawsuits carried on at the city's gates, prophetic oracles proclaimed in the marketplace, priestly rituals and liturgies recited in the sanctuary. There are scores of *Gattungen*, or literary forms, in the Old Testament and New Testament, each with its own *Sitz im Leben*, or life situation, and each performing its particular function. To many of these Gunkel was again able to adduce many striking parallels in the literatures of the other peoples with whose history and culture Israel and the early Christian community were closely related.

Gunkel's first major work, *Schöpfung und Chaos in Urzeit und Endzeit* (1895), was a religio-historical study of Genesis 1:1-2:4a and Revelation 12. The myth of the chaos dragon, present in both texts, was traced throughout the literatures of the ancient Near East and the Old and New Testament. The nature of myth was carefully described, and its transformation in the biblical records clearly set forth. A relatively short time later, in 1901, his great commentary on the Book of Genesis appeared in the "Göttinger Handkommentar zum Alten Testament." Here the scholar's interpretative and exegetical powers came to fruition. He not only demonstrated the validity of his methodology, but also made the ancient legends and traditions speak again in their original accents. In some respects the commentary has never been superseded. The introduction, *Die Sagen der Genesis*, was published separately and translated into English, and has appeared most recently in paperback with an introduction by W. F. Albright. While it shows a complete mastery of the critical problems of the book, it is primarily concerned with elucidating the features which mark the legend as a genre, the progress of the successive narratives, and the motifs which persist throughout.

Not long after the publication of the Genesis commentary, Gunkel was offered an opportunity to present an examplar of the literary history of Israel. In the volume on *Die orientalischen Literaturen* (1906) in Hinneberg's series *Die Kultur der Gegenwart*, he prepared a programmatic sketch of what he considered to be a proper literary history. It is a fascinating report, illuminated by acute insight into the types and forms of Israel's speech, by analysis and characterization of each *Gattung*, and by a revealing description of the concrete situation in daily life in which the *Gattung* had its place. A series of essays, *Reden und Aufsätze* (1913), some of which were drawn from previous publications, included a number of articles related to form criticism. Among them were "Fundamental Problems of Hebrew Literary History," (reprinted in *What Remains of the Old Testament* [1928]), "Egyptian Parallels to the Old Testament," and "The Close of Micah." A smaller work, *Das Märchen im Alten Testament* (1917), while not so well known as other works, traces the genre of the folktale and its prevailing motifs throughout the Old Testament, and again adduces many parallels drawn from the literatures of other peoples.

But perhaps the most impressive monument to Gunkel's contributions to biblical learning is the German encyclopedia bearing the title *Die Religion in Geschichte und Gegenwart* (1st ed., 1909-13). In 1910 he became one of its editors, and the second edition (1927-31) bears on its title page the names of Hermann Gunkel and Leopold Zscharnack. More than a hundred articles come from Gunkel, and the work as a whole bears the stamp of his religio-historical point of view. In both editions Gunkel contributed the article on the Psalms. Already in 1917 he had written a little book on selected Psalms, *Ausgewählte Psalmen*, and from that time on his attention centered more and more on the Psalter. In the period between the first and second editions of *RGG* he prepared a monumental commentary on the book (1926), and the companion introductory volume, *Einleitung in die Psalmen*, appeared the year after his death in 1932. Joachim Begrich, his devoted and accomplished pupil, saw the work to completion. It is in every way a masterly performance. In more than 450 large and closely-packed pages the literary features of each literary type are described in exhaustive detail. More than sixty pages are devoted to the Hymn alone, and every representative of the type, in other parts of the Old Testament and in the cognate literatures as well as in the Psalter itself, is cited.

The article on the Psalms given below is drawn from the second edition of *RGG* and provides a succinct and admirable synopsis of Gunkel's larger monumental work. *Multum in parvo!* For the reader who wishes to understand the nature of Hebrew poetic composition, its rhetoric and composition, its different literary genres and the style and structure which characterize each, this essay should prove rewarding. He will come to recognize and appreciate the distinctive qualities which mark each type, whether Hymn or song of Yahweh's enthronement, Community or Individual Lament, Thanksgiving Psalm or Royal Psalm, Liturgy or Torah, Blessing, or the fusion of several poetic types. But he will gain more because he will be able to enter into the devotional life of ancient Israel in a new way; he will sense the spirit which animates the worshiper as he enters into the divine presence on various occasions of celebration and festival; he will be listening to Israel's response to the divine revelation recorded in the other books of the Old Testament, and find himself perhaps participating in the ecstatic shouts of joy and praise, in petitions for forgiveness and healing, in prayers of contrition and confession, in historical recitals and rehearsals, in full-throated adorations and triumphant paeans. He will hear Israel singing, Israel in her most authentic moods, and will come to discern something of that which lay deepest in the soul of the pious suppliant and worshiper.

Gunkel recognized that the earliest psalms were all cultic in character, but he believed that many of them were later liberated from their cultic setting into spiritual songs and prayers. His student, Sigmund Mowinckel, took issue with him here. Mowinckel was convinced that all the psalms were cultic, and in six important monographs, entitled *Psalmenstudien* (1921-24), he sought not only to define their cultic provenience and *Sitz im Leben*, their cultic terminology and imagery, but also the occasions of celebration and festival, of mourning and lamentation, and their relation to other contexts in the life of ancient Israel. The second monograph of the Psalmenstudien, *Das Thronbesteigungsfest Jahwäs und der Ursprung der Eschatologie* (1920), a work of more than three hundred large pages, is one of the most influential and important contributions to our understanding of the Psalter. Like Gunkel's works, it is composed in an engaging and eminently readable style. Mowinckel followed Gunkel in his isolation of the *Gattung* of the psalm of the divine enthronement, but whereas Gunkel recognized only six specimens of this type (Pss. 47, 93, 96-99), Mowinckel found many more, in whole or in part, altogether about forty. He associated them with the annual celebration of the enthronement of Yahweh on the occasion of the New Year's festival and found in the Babylonian *akitu* celebrations the source of their composition and content. Thus the association of the chaos dragon conflict in the primeval abyss with the coronation of the king could be explained, Mowinckel contended, only by a common setting. While scholars today believe that he has overstated his case, many of them recognize the importance of his view and hold to it in a more or less modified form. It should be noted, too, that Mowinckel discussed in these hymns the origins of Israel's eschatology.

Other scholars too have departed from Gunkel in his classification of the literary types and have suggested alternative forms, such as the prayer of the falsely accused, emphasized by Hans Schmidt, in his *Das Gebet der Angeklagten in den Psalmen* (1928), or the hymns associated with the annual celebration of a royal festival on Mount Zion in which the election of David and the election of Jerusalem were celebrated, described by Hans-Joachim Kraus in his work *Die Königsherrschaft Gottes im Alten Testament* (1951) and his *Worship in Israel*

(1966). Kraus has also written a full-length commentary on the Psalms in the "Biblischer Kommentar" (1960), and while one is constantly aware of the presence of Hermann Gunkel, Kraus has taken account of the many contributions since Gunkel's day which have profited from archeological discoveries, new methodological procedures, and reinterpretations of the cultic life of ancient Israel. Type or form criticism is proving a great stimulus for our understanding of the theology of the Old and New Testaments; indeed, it is not too much to say that it has transformed our approach to the biblical records and has provided us with a deeper grasp of the nature of Israelite and early Christian mentality and faith, as we can see, *inter alia*, in the contributions of Gerhard von Rad and Rudolf Bultmann and their disciples.

JAMES MUILENBURG

San Francisco Theological Seminary
San Anselmo, California
April, 1967

Translator's Preface

THIS is a translation of Hermann Gunkel's article on the Psalms in the second edition of *Die Religion in Geschichte und Gegenwart* (abbreviated as *RGG²*). Since this article was a revision of Gunkel's original article in the first edition of *Die Religion in Geschichte und Gegenwart* (*RGG¹*), variations of any significance from *RGG¹* to *RGG²* have been noted in the first set of footnotes, numbered *a*, *b*, *c*, etc. The documentation in *RGG¹* and the variations in the cross referencing from the first edition to the second edition have been ignored for the most part. It may be noted that in *RGG²* Gunkel replaced some of the documentation with references to his *Einleitung in die Psalmen*, which began to appear in the interval between the publication of the first and second editions of *RGG*. The documentation in the *RGG²* article has been given in full in the translation. Since it is difficult, if not impossible, to determine whether the cross references in the article derive from Gunkel or from a house editor (or both), only those cross references have been retained which refer to articles by Gunkel himself. This meant sacrificing references to articles by such giants of scholarship as P. Volz, W. Baumgartner, K. Galling, J. Hempel, and R. Bultmann; but the names of the majority of authors cited have faded into obscurity. The footnotes numbered *1, 2, 3,* etc., contain the documentation and the cross references. All bracketed material in both sets of footnotes has been supplied by the translator.

Where passages from the Psalms are quoted in the text, the R.S.V. translation has been given. However, in those cases where Gunkel's rendering differs substantially from the R.S.V., his rendering has been translated in a footnote. Where verse numbers in the Hebrew Bible differ from those in the English Bible, the former have been given in parentheses or brackets following the English references.

The "List of Literary Types and Technical Terms" at the end of the book will give the reader some idea of how Gunkel's categories have been rendered into English.

While every effort has been made to give the reader an accurate picture of Gunkel's views in the original and revised articles, a full picture can be obtained only by reading the articles themselves.

THOMAS M. HORNER

Philadelphia Divinity School
Philadelphia, Pennsylvania
February, 1967

Contents

* The numbers in parentheses are the numbers of the sections in the German.

1

INTRODUCTION: THE SOURCES

SINCE a scholarly study is always a study of material in its context, the investigator who wishes to deal with any subject of major propor-tions has the task, first of all, of presenting an overview of all the material which belongs to his topic or is related to it in any way.[a] Therefore, it is not sufficient to deal only with the biblical book of Psalms,[1] where the great majority of psalms which originated in an-cient Israel are to be found;[b] rather, we are convinced from the outset that our presentation must include also those songs which do not belong to the Psalter, whether these are found in the Bible or, indeed, outside of Israel, insofar as they show any real inner relationship with the Psalms.

Such materials we now have in abundance. First of all, in the his-torical books of the Old Testament we have the Song of Hannah,[2]

[a] way. In doing so he must first disregard the more or less fortuitous context in which the materials have come down to us, and instead see them in their original context. Therefore

[b] found; rather, we must ask whether there are other psalms that have been preserved outside the Psalter. We are convinced

[1] "Psalterbuch" (Gunkel), RGG[2] 4, cols. 1628-30. [The article deals with the traditions concerning the composition of the Psalms and with the problem of the dating of the psalms, including the questions of whether they contain any definite historical references and whether any of the psalms are to be dated in the Maccabean period (Gunkel does not assign any of the psalms in the canoni-cal book to this late period).]

[2] [I Sam. 2:1-10.]

the Psalm of Jonah,[3] the Song of Hezekiah,[4] the Song of the Sea,[5] and others. These songs are intimately related to the Psalms and could stand just as well in the Psalter itself.[c]

The book of Job[6] also contains many lyrical compositions, even though the book as a whole belongs to another literary type.[d] But it is in the prophetic books, especially, that we find many compositions which are similar to the Psalms.[7] To be sure, Hebrew prophecy originally had nothing to do with religious lyric poetry; but[e] in the course of history the prophets took over the lyric form, as well as other literary forms, for the purpose of giving expression to their feelings or in order to make an impression upon their people, who were very receptive to poetry. For example, in anticipation of the joy of Israel on that day when Yahweh would deliver his people out of all distress, the prophets would compose a song of rejoicing for the community to sing in that last time. Such a song of rejoicing composed by the prophets has the same forms as those Hymns which have been handed down to us in the Psalter.[8] Or, in order to give moving expression to the lamentation of their people under foreign oppression and of their longing for deliverance, the prophets would sing, in the name of the people, a Lament after the pattern of those the community was accustomed to raise in the forecourt of the sanctuary in times of great distress.[9] Jeremiah especially—mocked, persecuted, and at the point of death—poured out his anguish in marvelous songs which are similar to the Laments

---

[c] itself. They found their way into the narrative books since the narrators were well aware of the pleasing effect that results when prose is interspersed with poetry.

[d] type. At many points, however, the poet of this book borrowed from religious lyric. For example, when he wants to portray Job's suffering or Job's protestations of innocence, he can find no better way than to have Job sing Laments or Songs of Innocence like those we find in the Psalter. And when he wishes to portray the majesty of God, he turns to the Hymn.

[e] but in the course of a history of which we can in some measure still obtain an overview the prophets

---

[3] [Jonah 2:3-9 (Heb., 2:3-10).] "Jonapsalm" (Gunkel), *RGG*[2] 3, cols. 369-70.

[4] [Isa. 38:10-20.]

[5] [Exod. 15:1-18.] "Mossessegen, Moseslied und Meerlied," 3 (Gunkel), *RGG*[2] 4, col. 247.

[6] "Hiobbuch," 7 (Gunkel), *RGG*[2] 2, col. 1929.

[7] "Propheten," IIB, 3m (Gunkel), *RGG*[2] 4, cols. 1552-54.

[8] Cf. below, chap. 3, sec. A, and chap. 5, sec. A.

[9] Cf. below, chap. 3, sec. B, and chap. 5, sec. B.

of the Individual in the Psalter. In the biblical book the Lamentations of Jeremiah, chapters one, two, and four are Funeral Dirges; thus they do not belong here. But chapters three and five very likely do; chapter three[f] contains the Lament of an Individual; chapter five, a Community Lament.

The poetry of the later period also offers rich material. We possess an abundance of scattered psalms in the Apocrypha. The songs in the books of Tobit and of Judith[10] may be mentioned, as well as lyrical compositions in the books of Baruch and Sirach,[11] in I Maccabees,[12] and elsewhere. The so-called Psalms of Solomon is an entirely post-canonical collection of psalms. And from certain of the Odes of Solomon[13] it is apparent[g] that the composition of psalms continued to be practiced and the old forms still employed.

From these post-canonical songs we can obtain a clear picture of the composition of psalms after the collection of psalms in the Psalter was concluded. From a period which is prior to the history of Israel we possess Babylonian and Egyptian songs.[14] The discovery of the Babylonian psalms, especially, has been the[h] most important event in decades for psalm research. For here we learn to recognize a kind of psalm composition, which, for all of the differences between the Baby-

---

[f] chapter three contains a Private Lament, chapter five, a Public Lament. On the distinction between Funeral Dirges and Laments, which are often confused by modern scholarship, see the article "Dichtung, profane im AT," Vol. 2, col. 49.

[g] apparent that the composition of psalms continued to be practiced in the Jewish community and the old forms still employed.

[h] the most important event for psalm research in the whole of the nineteenth century.

[10] [Tob. 13; cf. also Tob. 8:5 f., 8:15-17; Jth. 16:2-17.]

[11] [Baruch 3:9-4:4; 4:5-5:9; Sirach 42:15-43:33; 44:1-50:24; 51:1-12.]

[12] [I Macc. 3:3-9; 14:4-15.]

[13] "Salomo-Oden" (Gunkel), *RGG*[2] 5, cols. 87-90.

[14] For more information on the Babylonian songs, the reader may consult E. Ebeling's article "Babylonien," II, 10a, *RGG*[2] 1, col. 710; also H. Zimmern, *Babylonische Hymnen und Gebete* (2 vols.; Leipzig: Hinrichs, 1905-11); M. Jastrow, Jr., *Die Religion Babyloniens und Assyriens* (2 vols.; Giessen: Ricker, 1905-12), I, 393 ff.; II, 1 ff. [a briefer treatment, in English, is given in Jastrow's *The Religion of Babylonia and Assyria* (Boston: Ginn, 1898), pp. 294-311]. On the Egyptian songs, cf. A. Erman, *Aegyptische Religion* (Berlin: Reimer, [3]1909), pp. 79 ff., and his *Literature of the Ancient Egyptians*, trans. A. M. Blackman (New York: Dutton, 1927). On both see H. Gressmann, *Altorientalische Texte und Bilder zum Alten Testament* (Tübingen: Mohr, [2]1926), I, 12 f., 241 ff., as well as other publications.

lonian and Israelite religions, is closely related to the biblical psalms in the literary forms employed and in many of the ideas set forth; these Babylonian psalms preceded the lyric compositions of the Bible by centuries, indeed, in part by millennia.[1] Admittedly, only the commentaries of the most recent period have consulted the newly discovered Oriental texts.

If we now examine the Psalms in the light of the context outlined above, we see that in place of a single biblical book we have an important kind of religious poetry for which we possess, even outside the Psalter, an abundance of documents, and which we are able to trace from the third millennium B.C. to the time of the rise of Christianity, where we find it, for example, in the Gospel of Luke and in the Revelation of John,[15] until it is gradually superseded by the religious poetry of the Christian church, the post-Christian synagogue, and Gnosticism.

---

[1] millennia. It must be added, to be sure, that only a minute number of the scholars investigating the Psalms have showed themselves worthy recipients of this gift; commentaries on the Psalter, even the most recent ones, have almost completely ignored the Babylonian texts.

[15] [Luke 1:46-55; 1:68-79; 2:29-32; Rev. 4:8*b*; 4:11; 5:9 f.; 11:17 f.; 15:3 f.; 16:5-7.]

LITURGICAL POETRY

OUR next task is to bring some kind of order to this material, which takes such diverse forms and, in point of time, is spread out over so many centuries. In this process the investigator should seek to feel his way into the innate, natural structure of the whole body of material: he should make some sound basic observations, in accordance with which the material falls into a context, as if by itself.[j] The most important observation for the psalms is that some of them belong to poetry used in worship, while others do not presuppose the worship service. The conjecture can immediately be added, in accordance with the general course of the history of religions, and not only that of Israel, that those psalms which were composed for the cultus are, on the whole, older than those which the pious poet composed for his own use. Indeed, in the earliest history of man all religion existed only in the form of the worship service, while a cultless piety developed only later. This conjecture is supported also by Babylonian parallels, namely, the Babylonian psalm poetry. This Babylonian poetry, which, as a whole, precedes the Israelite, belongs to the context of the worship service. There is the further illustration, from the history of Protestant hymnody, that the "chorale" is older than the "spiritual song."

A word about Hebrew liturgical poetry is now in order. From time immemorial Israel's worship consisted of a vast number of ritual acts

[j] itself. To employ an image, our initial task is to do for psalm research what Linnaeus succeeded in doing for botany. The most important observation for the Psalms is that some of them, admittedly only a small fraction thereof, belong to the poetry used in the cult, while the majority do not presuppose the worship service. The conjecture

which one performed for God or in God's name. Such[k] acts, however, were generally accompanied by sacred words which elucidated them and, at the same time, reinforced their power. In the secular sphere the Work Song might serve as a comparison; this type of song was sung as the accompaniment to a particular kind of work. A parallel in the Christian sphere is the sacrament, in which word and act also belong together.[l] In Israel, for example, when the public service of worship was at an end, the priest, standing at the altar, lifted his hands over the people (Sir. 50:20) and spoke the venerable words of the Aaronic Benediction (Num. 6:22ff.).[16] Such words, which at that time were already frequently hoary[m] with age, generally possess poetic form, in much the same way as Incantations and Prophetic Sayings were originally cast in such forms. An example of such a rhythmic Incantation is this saying of Elisha[17]:

> The Lord's arrow of victory,
>> the arrow of victory over Syria!
>> (II Kings 13:17)

[n]Such cultic sayings were especially likely to be cast in poetic form if they were to be spoken by an entire community. For only through song could a large group of people express itself in an orderly manner in antiquity. Furthermore, as would follow from the greater emotional

[k] Such acts, however, as many passages tell us and as lies in the nature of the case, were generally accompanied

[l] together. In Israel, for example, when a body was discovered in the open country and the identity of the murderer was not known, the elders of the neighboring villages assembled, the neck of a heifer was broken, and the people washed their hands over the heifer, saying, "Our hands did not shed this blood, neither did our eyes see it shed" (Deut. 21). Or when the holy act of the public service of worship was at an end

[m] hoary with age and possessed definite form, generally

[n] One might also cite the incantation at the well, in Numbers 21:17 f. Such cultic sayings were especially likely to be cast in poetic form if they were to be spoken by an entire community, by a choir or a congregation. For only through song can a large group of people express itself in an orderly manner; this is why we still have congregational singing in our churches, even though men [i.e., males] today are not in the habit of singing in secular life. Now, this ancient type of cult singing is vastly different from anything to be found in our society in that it is characterized by the much greater naïveté and emotional capacities of the people of that day. The people did not sit peacefully in pews, as we do; they jumped and danced, they were jubilant, they shouted, with intoxicating music

[16] "Aaronitischer Segen" (Gunkel), *RGG*[2] 1, col. 2.
[17] "Elisa" (Gunkel), *RGG*[2] 2, cols. 112-13.

capacities of the people of that day, this type of cult singing is vastly different from anything to be found in our society. As they sang they were jubilant or in lamentation; they shouted or wailed; they danced or rolled in the dust, with intoxicating music providing both rhythm and melody. A performance of such a Cult Song is described in these lines:

> [For I once] went with the throng,
>> and led them in procession to the house of God,
> with glad shouts and songs of thanksgiving,
>> a multitude keeping festival.[18]
>>
>> (Ps. 42:4; [Heb., 42:5])

Compare also the descriptions in Exodus 15:20; 32:6, 17 f.; II Samuel 6:5; and Nehemiah 12:27 ff.

°We are able to piece together a rather clear picture of such Cult

° Not many such Cult Songs have been handed down to us, but we are nonetheless able to piece together a rather clear picture of them. To do so we must combine the following: (a) remarks—in historical books or in laws—which describe the settings of these sayings; (b) borrowings and imitations of the ancient style, in the Psalms, the prophets, and in Job; (c) those songs in the Psalter in which the accompanying action still shows through clearly. Where cultic acts are portrayed in the material handed down to us, we have to ask what words or songs accompanied their performance. Where songs have been transmitted to us, we have to guess at the acts with which they were once associated.

Both act and word are given in Numbers 10:35 f. When the ark was lifted up, the song went:

Arise, O Lord, and let thy enemies be scattered;
>> and let them that hate thee flee before thee.

In the evening, when the ark was returned to rest, the song went:

Return, O Lord, to the ten thousand thousands of Israel.
[Gunkel's rendering:
Return to rest ($\check{s}^e\underline{b}ah$), Yahweh,
>> in the camp ($b^e ri\underline{b}'o\underline{t}$) of the clans of Israel.]

These words give us the pattern of a Cult Song; word and

18 [Gunkel's rendering in *RGG*[1] reads:
how I went to the tabernacle and danced (*'eddaddeh*?)
>> my way to the house of Yahweh,
with loud shouts of joy and thanksgiving,
>> amid the high-spirited tumult.
[His rendering in *RGG*[2] reads:
For I once went to the "Tent of the Majestic One" [*Zelt des Herrlichen*],
to Yahweh's house,
amid the sound of rejoicing and thanksgiving,
>> amid the "clamor" of the pilgrims.]

Songs, especially when we are informed of both the action and the accompanying words. We have an example in a song which was used when the ark was lifted up:

> Arise, O Lord, and let thy enemies be scattered;
>> and let them that hate thee flee before thee.
>>> (Num. 10:35)

These words give us the pattern of a Cult Song; word and act are so closely bound together that one without the other is inconceivable.

Psalm 24 provides an example of a song in which the action is easy to supply:

> Lift up your heads, O gates!
>> and be lifted up, O ancient doors!
>> that the King of glory may come in.
>>> (24:7)

This verse was sung by a choir which stood before the doors of the temple seeking entry. It is also quite clear that God himself is in their midst and that they are celebrating his entrance. By what symbolic means God is represented here, however, we learn from what follows. For now, on the inside, another choir answers in the name of the doors:

> Who is the King of glory?
>> (24:8a)

Whereupon we have the answer, which mentions Yahweh by name and praises him as glorious in battle. The whole thing is then repeated (vss. 9-10),[p] and as a final note Yahweh's cult name is proclaimed:

> The Lord of hosts,
> he is the King of glory!
>> (24:10b)

Yahweh Ṣeḇā'ôṯ,[19] the God of war, had as his symbol the ark. Thus, in all probability we may think here of a festival in which the ark, following a battle, is returned to the temple on Zion.[q]

Other passages which have to do with an "entrance" are Psalms 100:2 ("Serve the Lord with gladness! Come into his presence with

---

[p] (vss. 9-10)—in the Israelite cult, as well as in the Babylonian cult, such repetition is a favorite method of expressing sublime solemnity—and as a final
[q] Zion; the Babylonians also had such entrance festivals.

[19] "Zebaoth" (Gunkel), *RGG*[2] 5, cols. 2085-86.

singing!") ; 100:4; and 95:1-7*a*. Isaiah 26:1 introduces a song which was sung to accompany an "entrance" ("Open the gates, that the righteous nation which keeps faith may enter in").

In addition to these entrance songs, there were the songs sung on pilgrimages. At that time people from the villages, small towns, and country districts went on pilgrimages together, and naturally there was singing along the way. For example:

> You shall have a song as in the night when a holy feast is kept; and gladness of heart, as when one sets out to the sound of the flute to go to the mountain of the Lord, to the Rock of Israel.[20]

> (Isa. 30:29)

The last three lines are taken from such a Pilgrim Song.

When a prophet wanted to depict the heathen's conversion to Yahweh, he presented a picture of the pilgrimage which they would make to Zion and then, in anticipation of that day, began to sing the song they would sing:

> Come, let us go up to the mountain of the Lord,
>   to the house of the God of Jacob.
>
> (Isa. 2:3; also Mic. 4:2)

According to Isaiah 30:29 (cited above) songs were also sung on a watch night [*Weihnacht*] during a vigil. For, by what better means could one shorten the long night than by singing, and what better subject could one choose at a holy festival than Yahweh's honor?

> Come, bless the Lord,
>   all you servants of the Lord,
> who stand by night in the house of the Lord.
>
> (Ps. 134:1)

[20] [Gunkel's rendering in *RGG*[1] reads:
  You shall have a song
      as in the night when the feast is kept,
  and gladness of heart,
      like that of the pilgrim singing to the sound of the flute
  as he comes to the mountain of Yahweh,
      to the Rock of Israel.
[His rendering in *RGG*[2]:
  You shall have a song
  as in the night
      when the "festal dancer" consecrates "*ḥôgēg*" [the festival],
  and gladness of heart like that of the pilgrim singing to the sound of
      the flute
      as he comes to the mountain of Yahweh, to the Rock of Israel.]

3

LITURGICAL POETRY AND
ITS "SETTING IN LIFE"

HOW are we to distinguish the various types of Cult Songs? It should go without saying that we do it always according to their "setting in life," that is, according to the various situations in which the songs were sung.[r] The principal literary types are represented by those songs which were sung on the most frequently recurring occasions. A common setting in life is thus one of the distinguishing characteristics of songs belonging to the same literary type. Another distinguishing characteristic is the great number of thoughts and moods which these songs share, while yet another—a very distinctive characteristic—is the literary forms [*Formensprache*] which are prevalent in them.[21] Accordingly, we are able to distinguish four main types.

A. HYMNS

First of all, there is the Hymn, a song of praise (Hebrew *t^ehillāh*, which is derived from the verb *hillēl*, meaning "to sing a hymn"). Hymns were sung on holy days at the solemn sacrifice (Amos 5:21 ff. connects festivals, sacrifices, songs, and harp playing[s]). The oldest example which we have of this type is the Song of Miriam:[22]

> Sing to the Lord, for he has triumphed gloriously;
> the horse and the rider he has thrown into the sea.
>> (Exod. 15:21)

[r] [The next three sentences are not in *RGG*[1].]
[s] playing, and Hosea 9:1 speaks of Hymns which were sung at the threshing floors during the harvest festival). The oldest

[21] "Literaturgeschichte, biblische," 2b (Gunkel), *RGG*[2] 3, cols. 1677 f.
[22] "Mirjam" (Gunkel), *RGG*[2] 4, col. 30.

We also have the Song of Deborah,[23] which begins like an introduction to a Hymn: "to the Lord I will sing" (Judg. 5:3). Many Hymns are found in the prophets, especially in the Second Isaiah (e.g., 40:12 ff., 22 ff.; 44:23, 24 ff.; 45:8; *et al.*). The oldest of these by far is the Hymn of the Seraphim:

> Holy, holy, holy is the Lord of hosts;
>> the whole earth is full of his glory.
>>> (Isa. 6:3)

In the Psalter itself we also have some very early Hymns, such as Psalm 19:1-6 (Heb., 19:2-7) and Psalm 29. All of these compositions agree in content and form in so many ways that we are able to piece together a rather distinct picture of the early Hymn.

The basic form of the earliest Hymn, as well as the primitive core of the singing of the Hymn, is the word "Hallelujah."[24] In later times this is still to be found as the acclamation of the congregation at the end (or at the beginning) of Hymns. That we attach importance to beginnings and endings[t] may be explained by the fact that they are a distinguishing mark of literary works in general, but especially of those in Israel. Very frequently the Hebrew Hymn will begin: "Give praise," "Sing" (Exod. 15:21), "Give thanks" (Ps. 105:1, etc.). These phrases were originally the precentor's address to the choir.[u] Then the hymn proceeds as the precentor invokes God's name ("Praise Yahweh" or "Sing to Yahweh")[v] and at the same time addresses the singers, who are variously called "you righteous ones" (Ps. 33:1), "daughter of Zion" (Zeph. 3:14; Zech. 2:10 [Heb., 2:14]; 9:9), and on a grander scale: "you peoples" (Ps. 47:1 [Heb., 47:2]), "all the earth" (Pss. 66:1; 100:1; 98:4), "sea," "coastlands," and "deserts" (Isa. 42:10 ff.), "heavens," "mountains," and "forest" (Isa. 44:23; Ps. 96:11 f.).[w] Another form of the introduction presupposes that a particular person is singing: "to the Lord I will sing" (Judg. 5:3; cf. Ps. 34:1 [Heb., 34:2]). This kind of beginning is also attested in Babylonian material

---

t ["and endings" is not in *RGG*[1].]

u choir, or the choir's address to itself.

v [The references to God's name are missing in *RGG*[1].]

w 96:11 f.). "Sing to him a new song" was once quite novel; later, it was frequently repeated (Pss. 33:3; 96:1; Isa. 42:10). Another form

---

23 "Debora" (Gunkel), *RGG*[2] 1, col. 1800.
24 "Hallelujah" (Gunkel), *RGG*[2] 2, col. 1592.

(e.g., "I will sing of the struggles of the gods"), where it also derives from the cult, for it is sung by a priest or a worshiper in the sanctuary.

Next, the main part, or body, of the Hymn contains the *t*ᵉ*hillōṯ*, that is, the attributes and deeds of God which evoke the praise. Here the following forms are customary. First, the *t*ᵉ*hillōṯ* may be added to the introduction in the form of a series of participles, which, in English grammar, would be represented by relative clauses, as in this classic example:

> who forgives all your iniquity,
>> who heals all your diseases,
> who redeems your life from the Pit,
>> who crowns you with steadfast love and mercy.
>
> (Ps. 103:3-4)

Or, the *t*ᵉ*hillōṯ* may be expressed in separate sentences, in which Yahweh himself, his deeds, his creative works, or his attributes are the subject; e.g., "Holy, holy, holy is the Lord of hosts" (Isa. 6:3). Also popular is the form of the rhetorical question: "Who is like thee, O Lord, among the gods?" (Exod. 15:11). The hymns speak of Yahweh in the second or third person. Less frequent is the form in which God proclaims his own praise. One finds this form now and then in Babylonian poems, e.g., in this Ishtar Psalm:

> Rejoicing in the highest, rejoicing in the highest,
>> as a goddess I go forth.[25]

ˣThere is an imitation of this style in the majestic speeches of Yahweh in Job 38 ff.

The subjects of the Yahweh Hymns are the following. There is Yahweh's manifestation in the terror of the volcano, earthquake, thunder, and storm (an example is Ps. 29), surely a very ancient element in Israelite hymnody. Furthermore, there is Yahweh's creative power (as in the Second Isaiah, Job, and Ps. 104); that this material is very old is shown by the Babylonian and Egyptian parallels,[26] as well as by

---

ˣ In the performance of the rite, the priest, clothed as a deity, may have spoken such words. There is an imitation

[25] H. Zimmern, *Babylonische Hymnen und Gebete* (see n. 14 above), II, 22.

[26] Cf., e.g., the "Hymn to the Sun" of Amenophis IV, which bears an affinity to Ps. 104; see H. Gressmann's article, "Aegypten," III, 3, *RGG*² 1, cols. 108-09. [There is a translation of the hymn, by John A. Wilson, in J. Pritchard (ed.), *Ancient Near Eastern Texts Relating to the Old Testament* (Princeton: University Press, ²1955), pp. 369-71.]

the abundance of archaic mythological conceptions which find expression in this type of poem. Then, there is the abode of the deity in the heavens—another notion which was well-known among the surrounding peoples. Not least,[y] there is Yahweh's powerful and beneficent sovereignty over mankind, his constant concern for his people and for the faithful (Deut. 33:26 ff.). It was especially popular, also, to sing of his deeds in the past, even as Babylonian and Egyptian hymns are filled with allusions to myths. The Israelite Hymns sometimes praise Yahweh's victory over the chaos dragon, most beautifully of all in Psalm 89:10 ff. (Heb., 89:11 ff.).

The[z] predominant mood in all the Hymns is the enthusiastic but reverent adoration of the glorious and awe-inspiring God. To a certain extent, it might be said that the purpose of the Hymns was to give pleasure to Yahweh, whom they extol with such exuberance. For just as the king at a festive meal would not dispense with songs sung in his praise, so Yahweh was offered songs whenever one celebrated his festivals or offered him sacrifice. But also for the singers themselves the songs were beneficial. The religious idea, when expressed vocally, became stronger, and the individual[a] was caught up in the mood of the throng (Ps. 40:5 [Heb., 40:6]).

B. COMMUNITY LAMENTS

One does not always sing praises and give thanks; there is also a time to grieve and lament. Alongside the happy festivals of rejoicing in the community stand the days of lamentation. When crop failure, pestilence, and danger from the enemy afflicted the people, such a day of lamentation was observed. On such occasions all the people would assemble at the sanctuary, tear their clothes, fast, weep, lament, and sound the trumpet. In this manner a passionate people would implore their God to have mercy upon them. This description is taken from the book of Joel, whose first two chapters contain an actual liturgy which has to do with a disastrous locust plague. Elsewhere similar days of lamentation are depicted.[b] Such days of mourning are presupposed in

[y] [The next clause is not in *RGG*[1].]

[z] The predominant mood in all the Hymns is enthusiasm for the glory of Yahweh, and the purpose of the Hymns is to give pleasure

[a] the individual was caught up in the enthusiasm of the throng. Therefore such occasions, when the whole community joined in the Hymns with gusto, could be great experiences for the individual, who would look back on them with longing (Ps. 42:5).

[b] [This sentence is missing in *RGG*[1].]

historical sources, especially in the old Naboth narrative (I Kings 21:9 ff.; cf. also I Sam. 7:6) and in the prophets (Amos 5:16; Isa. 22:12; 29:4; 32:11 f.; Jer. 14:2; etc.). Thus, they were already customary from the earliest time. Songs which were sung on such occasions we call Community Laments.[c] These we have in Psalms 44; 60:1-5 (Heb., 60:3-7); 74; 79; 80; 89:38 ff. (Heb., 89:39 ff.), and 94.

The age of this particular type can be attested by the imitations found in the prophets. When they wanted to capture the mood of that day on which Israel would finally see the errors of its ways and repent of its sins, the prophets would sing such a Lament in anticipation of that time. Jeremiah furnishes us with a classic example:

> Behold, we come to thee;
>> for thou art the Lord our God.
>
> . . . .
> Let us lie down in our shame
>> and let our dishonor cover us;[27]
> For we have sinned against the Lord our God.
>> (Jer. 3:22*b*, 25*a,b*)

Other examples are found in Hosea 6:1-3; 14:3 f. (Heb., 14:4 f.); Isaiah 59:9 ff.; 64:7 ff. (Heb., 64:6 ff.); Jeremiah 14:7 ff., and 14:19 ff. Chapter five of the Lamentations of Jeremiah[28] is also a community Lament.[d] We may distinguish two sub-classes within this type, depending on whether the people confess their sins and ask forgiveness or whether they protest their innocence and try to persuade God to recognize it as well. The first class we call Pentitential Prayers of the Community[e] and the second, Confessions of Innocence of the Community,[f] of which Psalm 44 is an example.

In the prophetic literature[29] a Community Lament is customarily divided into two parts: (a) a passionate appeal, and (b) the divine response. In the book of Psalms the counterpart to the second element is the poet's "certainty of a hearing," which is an expression of his

[c] call Public Laments.

[d] a Public Lament.

[e] Public Penitential Prayers and the second,

[f] Public Confessions of Innocence, of which

[27] In penitential prayer the suppliant lies in the dust; cf. Ps. 44:25 (Heb., 44:26); Isa. 29:4.

[28] "Klagelieder Jeremiae" (Gunkel), *RGG²* 3, cols. 1049-52.

[29] Cf. below, chap. 5, sec. E.

confidence that his prayer will be heard. Its appearance in the psalm is often quite sudden and unmotivated. Accordingly, it may perhaps be supposed that on the days of lamentation in the earliest period the prayer was first uttered, whereupon the answer was proclaimed by the priest in God's name.[g]

Among the extant Babylonian and Egyptian poems there appear to be no such Community Laments. There the Hymns also contain no address to the people—a major distinction from the Israelite psalms, in which the community plays such an important role.[h]

C. Songs[i] of the Individual

[j]Next come the liturgical songs which were sung by pious individuals. But first we must ask whether there ever were such Songs of the Individual in Israel. Ever since the appearance of Rudolf Smend's article, "Ueber das Ich der Psalmen,"[30] the view has frequently been expressed among scholars that the "I" which so often appears in the Psalms is, perhaps, not the individual at all but the personification of the community. However, such a personification in the first person is possible only in cases in which intense suffering [*Pathos*] is experienced (e.g., Lam. 1:9, 11-16, 18f., *et al.*) and is to be assumed only in places where the poet says so expressly (e.g., Ps. 129:1) or where it is undoubtedly demanded by the sense (e.g., Mic. 7:7 ff.; Isa. 21:10; Ps. Sol. 1). Unless these indications are present (and they are infrequent), then the explanation of the "I" as the poet himself is the preferable one; indeed it is the natural and self-evident explanation.

The poetry of Jeremiah, which contains the same literary types as the "I" songs of the Psalter, supports this point of view; for here the "I" is Jeremiah himself, that is, an individual. One may also adduce

[g] name. This would correspond to Babylonian liturgies.

[h] [These two sentences are not in *RGG*[1].]

[i] [At the beginning of the article in *RGG*[1] this heading is given as "Prayers of the Individual."]

[j] In ancient Israel we hear less frequently of Cult Songs sung by pious individuals. This gap in our tradition is easily explained: our sources for the ancient period are almost exclusively historical books, which are concerned with the history of the community, or prophets, who are also strongly political in their orientation and address themselves not to the individual, but to the community. This is why we hear relatively little about the life of the individual in the earlier period. But were there ever such Songs of

[30] *Zeitschrift für die alttestamentliche Wissenschaft*, 8 (1888), 49-147.

the book of Job,[31] where such "I" psalms are placed in the mouth of Job, again an individual. One may cite, further, the superscriptions of the psalms ascribed to David, especially those for which a specific occasion for the composition of the song has been added, for these at least prove that the editors applied the "I" to the situation of an individual. Thus we sometimes read that a psalm is "The prayer of one afflicted, when he is faint and pours out his complaint before the Lord" (Ps. 102, superscription [Heb., 102:1]). Into this category should be placed the psalms attributed to Hannah, Jonah,[32] Hezekiah, and Manasseh (see the "Prayer of Manasseh" in the Apocrypha); thus, these were understood to have been connected with individuals. It is quite clear, also, that Sirach intended his "I" songs, e.g.,[k] the Thanksgiving Psalm in 51:1 ff., to be in his own name, in the same way as the Song of Mary (Luke 1:46 ff.) is understood to be in hers.[l] Of particular importance in this respect is the fact that the Babylonian Laments also surely have reference to individuals; occasionally there is a blank left in the Lament, where the worshiper is expected to supply his own name.

In addition to the foregoing considerations, we should take into account the great number of personal references found in these psalms in the Psalter, especially those in which the "I" clearly differentiates himself from other Israelites: "Thou hast caused my companions to shun me" (Ps. 88:8 [Heb., 88:9]); "I have become a stranger to my brethren" (Ps. 69:8 [Heb., 69:9;]); "For my father and my mother have forsaken me" (Ps. 27:10); "I have been old and now am young" (Ps. 37:25); "From thee comes my praise in the great congregation" (Ps. 22:25 [Heb., 22:26]; cf. also Pss. 26:12; 35:18; 40:10 [Heb., 40:11]; 52:9 [Heb., 52:11]; 111:11; 116:14). In these and in many other places an allegorical interpretation of the "I" would result in a very unnatural understanding of the psalm. Thus we maintain that, apart from a few isolated cases, the "I" almost invariably refers to the individual, and that therefore we have in the Psalms a rich collection

---

[k] e.g., the allegorical love story in 51:13 ff. and the Thanksgiving Psalm in

[l] hers, and the "I" songs in the Odes of Solomon (apart from the "Christ Songs") are to be understood as songs of an individual. Of particular importance in this respect is the fact that the Babylonian "I" songs, in which one finds the same categories as in the Hebrew, also surely have reference

---

[31] "Hiobbuch" (see n. 6 above).
[32] "Jonapsalm" (see n. 3 above).

of poetry of the individual.ᵐ The current explanation of the "I" as standing for the community is nothing more than a stubborn remnant of the allegorical interpretation of Scripture which prevailed in an earlier day.[33]

D. THANK OFFERING SONGS

A further breakdown of the various types of poems of the individual should also be made; the roots of these literary types reach down into the cult. The first of these is the Thank Offering Song (Hebrew, *tôḏāb*). A person is saved out of great distress—the shipwrecked man who is fortunate enough to be brought to land, the prisoner who is liberated, and especially the sick person who is restored to health—and now with grateful heart he brings a thank offering to Yahweh; it was customary that at a certain point in the sacred ceremony he would offer a song in which he expresses his thanks. We have such a Thank Offering Song in Psalm 66:13-14:

> I will come into thy house with burnt offerings;
>> I will pay thee my vows,
> that which my lips have uttered
>> and my mouth promised when I was in trouble.

The Psalm of Jonah is to be interpreted in the same way:

> But I with the voice of thanksgiving
>> will sacrifice to thee;
> what I have vowed I will pay.
>> (Jonah 2:9 [Heb., 2:10])

And in the Psalter again:

> I will offer to thee the sacrifice of thanksgiving
>> and call on the name of the Lord.
>> (Ps. 116:17)

The scene which we must try to visualize is something like this. The person who is to offer the sacrifice prostrates himself before the temple (Ps. 138:2). A number of relatives and acquaintances who expect to

ᵐ individual. From Ps. 91 one can see how fully developed individualism was at that time. The current

[33] Cf. E. Balla, *Das Ich der Psalmen* (Göttingen: Vandenhoeck & Ruprecht, 1912), and the literature cited there.

participate in the sacred meal stand around him (Ps. 22:26 [Heb., 22:27]). Then, with a sacred goblet in his hands (Ps. 116:13), and prior to the actual sacrifice, he sings his song with a loud voice:

> I will pay my vows to the Lord
>> in the presence of all his people,
> in the courts of the house of the Lord,
>> in your midst, O Jerusalem.
>>> (Ps. 116:18-19)

The body of such Thank Offering Songs contains a description of the singer's own recent fate. He may turn first to the bystanders and say something to this effect: "Listen, this is the way it was with me; so now thank Yahweh with me!" The principal ingredients of his explanation are the report of his distress, of his prayer to Yahweh, and of his deliverance. We have an example of this in the Psalm of Jonah:

> I called to the Lord, out of my distress,
>> and he answered me;
> out of the belly of Sheol I cried,
>> and thou didst hear my voice.
>
> . . . .
>
> When my soul fainted within me,
>> I remembered the Lord;
> and my prayer came to thee,
>> into thy holy temple.
>>> (Jonah 2:2, 7 [Heb., 2:3, 8])

In these songs we have the picture—very commonplace in our literature—of the worshiper[n] who has already passed through the underworld itself (although originally such a picture may have derived from a primitive background, perhaps referring to one who had been unconscious and was revived, as in Pss. 18:4 f. [Heb., 18:5 f.]; 30:3 [Heb., 30:4]; 40:2; Sirach 51:2 f., 9; *et al.*).

The Thank Offering Song concludes with the confession—the product of the worshiper's experience—that deliverance is wrought by Yahweh (Jonah 2:9 [Heb., 2:10] is an example).

---

[n] the worshiper who has already been dead, indeed has passed through the underworld itself, an image that may be mythological in origin (one thinks, e.g., of Tammuz); examples are Pss. 18:4 f.

A common Thank Offering Song, according to Jeremiah 33:11, was the verse:

> Give thanks to the Lord of hosts,
>> for the Lord is good,
>> for his steadfast love endures forever!

Psalm 100:4 f. also contains this verse, somewhat enlarged, in a poem which has been expressly entitled "A Psalm for the Thank Offering." This verse is also found in Psalms 106:1; 107:1; 118:1; and 136:1; and in these, also, the original poem has later been enlarged.[o] Furthermore, the antiquity of the short Thanksgiving Song contained in Jeremiah 33:11 cannot be disputed. Arguing in support of the great antiquity of this entire literary type is the fact that the Egyptian inscriptions and the Phoenician votive tablets,[p] as well as the so-called Babylonian "Job Psalm" (which is really a Thanksgiving Song), contain the same narrative structure.[34] One can see from such examples that in the case of this type of cultic poem we are not dealing with distinctively Israelite structures but with a type of poetic composition that was shared with the nations surrounding Israel and was certainly practiced in Israel from earliest times.

E. Laments of the Individual

Just as the Thanksgiving Songs of the Individual and the Community Hymns are counterparts, so we have standing alongside the Community Laments the cultic Laments of the Individual.[q] However, we possess among the Psalms very many Laments that are non-cultic in form, about which we shall have more to say later on.[35] This literary type has a very pronounced style: almost invariably the same thoughts and images recur. The peculiar and recurring situation in this psalm type

[o] enlarged; accordingly, we may expect to find elsewhere as well that compositions from an earlier period turn up in later Psalms. Furthermore, the antiquity

[p] [The next two clauses, "as . . . Song)," are not in *RGG1*.]

[q] Individual. As fate would have it, examples of this literary type have not been transmitted in the canon. Nevertheless, what we have uncovered thus far puts us in a position to sketch a fairly clear picture of these Laments. We possess among

[34] Cf. H. Gunkel, *Einleitung in die Psalmen* (Göttingen: Vandenhoeck & Ruprecht, 1933), secs. 7, 11, 12.

[35] Cf. below, chap. 5, sec. D.

is that of the suppliant who, in the midst of some illness which is a matter of life and death, must at the same time complain about his many enemies who are persecuting and slandering him. Most of these psalmists, moreover, assert their innocence—as happens in the Psalms of Innocence—and curse their enemies, as in the Imprecatory Psalms. Others acknowledge their guilt and ask forgiveness, as in the Penitential Psalms. The order in many of these psalms is a characteristic one: first, the wailing, almost desperate lament and the passionate prayer; then, suddenly, the certainty of deliverance in a jubilant/tone (Ps. 22 is a classic example).[r]

But originally this literary type, too, derives from the worship service, a fact which Sigmund Mowinckel, especially, has called to our attention.[36] It is demonstrated by the many allusions to the time and place of the performance of the psalm, the dress and behavior of the suppliant, and so on (cf. Pss. 5:3, 7 [Heb., 5:4, 8]; 28:2; 38:6 [Heb., 38:7]; 42:8 [Heb., 42:9]; 88:13 [Heb., 88:14]; *et al.*). Hence, if we wish to uncover the original form of these songs, we must, following the pattern in other psalm types, search out those cultic acts to which these songs must have belonged at one time. The cultic acts we consider must be those that were performed in connection with sickness.

Sickness, especially that of a very serious nature, was, according to the belief of ancient Israel, definitely something "sent from God," a divine punishment.[37] This explains why there were religious acts and songs associated with illness. As we have seen, in these psalms two basic but distinct moods are manifest: either the suppliant considers himself innocent—in which case he says, "Acknowledge my righteousness!"—or he realizes his guilt and prays, "Forgive my sins!" But in either case his prayer reads, "Save me! Help me!" Therefore, if a sacred act accompanied these songs originally, it might be reconstructed as follows. The sick man would appear in the sanctuary in order to obtain healing. There, however, sacred acts must have taken place in which, in response to his prayer, he is absolved of his sin (such forgiveness is assumed in the Penitential Psalms), or in which he attests his innocence, as in the Psalms of Innocence.

That this interpretation is substantially correct is indicated by certain images in the psalms themselves. It is a well-known fact that poetic

---

[r] [The next two sentences are not in *RGG*[1].]

[36] Cf. S. Mowinckel, *Psalmenstudien* (6 vols.; Kristiana: Dybwad, 1921-24).
[37] "Leiden," II, 1 (Gunkel), *RGG*[2] 3, col. 1562.

imagery is very often derived from an actual occurrence. Thus we are told in this Pentitential Psalm:

> Purge me with hyssop, and I shall be clean;
> wash me, and I shall be whiter than snow.
> (Ps. 51:7 [Heb., 51:9])

The action which is mentioned here only figuratively—the washing and the sprinkling—originally was an actual occurrence and was done in order to bring about the cleansing of the sinner and the healing of his sickness. Thus, we have here the rite, or one of the rites, from one of the oldest Pentitential Psalms.[s] Just how ancient such expiation and pentitential rites are can be shown from passages like Isaiah 6:6 f. and Job 1:5. Indeed, their antiquity is attested by the nature of the case itself. As further evidence that our reconstruction is correct, we have the Babylonian Laments, which in their basic structure and in many details are closely related to those of Israel; the connection of these Babylonian Laments with all kinds of expiatory acts can be demonstrated.[38] Accordingly,[t] we may regard as very ancient those psalms (as well as those sections found in the non-cultic Laments preserved in the Psalter) which have parallels in the corresponding Babylonian literature and which, by their very nature, would accord well with the cultic psalm. Here belongs the solemn invocation of God which introduces such psalms, and which is a necessary ingredient of every prayer; then, in the body of the song, the wailing laments or prayers of supplication; and, finally, at the end the vow[u] that upon recovery a glorious Thanksgiving Psalm will be offered. This certainty of a hearing, which is very prominent toward the conclusion of the Israelite Lament Psalms, we shall explain as we did those found in the corresponding[v] Community Laments[39]: they constitute a substitute for the original priestly absolution. The principal difference between the Babylonian and the

---

[s] Psalms. Another custom is presupposed in this Psalm of Innocence: "I wash my hands in innocence, and go about thy altar, O Lord" (Ps. 26:6); the worshiper's actions here testify to his innocence (Deut. 21:6; Matt. 27:24). Just how ancient

[t] Accordingly, we may regard as very ancient those sections found

[u] the vow, very common both in Hebrew and Babylonian Psalms, that upon

[v] corresponding Public Laments

---

[38] [See, e.g., the Shurpu text in I. Mendelsohn (ed.), *Religions of the Ancient Near East: Sumero-Akkadian Religious Texts and Ugaritic Epics* (New York: Liberal Arts Press, 1955), pp. 211-14.]

[39] Cf. above, chap. 3, sec. B.

Israelite Laments consists in the fact that in the one a polytheistic framework is taken for granted, whereas in the other only Yahweh is acknowledged. In addition, the Babylonian Laments are filled with magic, while in the extant biblical songs magic is completely lacking[w] or, at least, has receded far into the background.

F. ENTRANCE LITURGIES, TORAH SONGS, AND BLESSINGS

In addition to these major literary types, there are some minor ones. First, the Liturgy of Entrance. Examples are Psalms 15; 24:3-6; and Isaiah 33:14-16. Note the uniform construction. First comes the question of who will be allowed to approach the holy place; then the answer, which enumerates the particular requirements; and, finally, the declaration of a blessing. The performance of this liturgy may be visualized as follows. The layman, who is about to enter the sanctuary, inquires of the priest, "What is required of me that I might enter here?" The priest then gives the answer, in which the requirements of the deity are stipulated. Then, according to his priestly prerogative, he adds the blessing.

Utilizing this form the prophets painted a vivid picture of the conversion of sinners in the last times: when Yahweh's terrible judgment comes upon the enemies of Zion, then within the city itself sinners shall tremble before this awesome God and, approaching the sanctuary, will anxiously inquire, as one does in a Liturgy of Entrance, who will be allowed to remain in the holy places.

Related to the Liturgy of Entrance is the Torah Interrogation,[x] of which Micah 6:6-8 contains an imitation: the penitent appears before the holy place and, mentioning a number of possible expiations, inquires of the oracle by what means he may atone for his guilt, whereupon the oracle indicates what is required in this particular case.[40] Parallels may be found in the Babylonian materials.[41]

Finally, the pronouncements of the Blessing and of the Curse at one time also accompanied the performance of sacred acts.

---

[w] lacking but in the earlier Israelite cultic poetry may have played some sort of role.

[x] the Torah Song, of which

---

[40] "Leiden," II, 2 (see n. 37 above), col. 1562.
[41] Cf. H. Zimmern, *Beiträge zur babylonischen Religion*, I (1896), 2 ff.

G. ROYAL PSALMS

Related to the cultic poetry and yet constituting a special group are the Royal Psalms. That such psalms existed and that they bore a religious stamp should not surprise us, for everywhere among ancient peoples the king stood in some sort of relationship with the deity. We know that there were royal temples in Jerusalem, Bethel, and Dan. In those temples on solemn occasions the prince himself offered sacrifices and allowed others to offer sacrifices for him. Thus, it is obvious that prayer was offered for him or in his name. In fact, we possess such Royal Psalms from Egypt and Babylonia.[42]

Royal Psalms in the Old Testament are Psalms 2, 18, 20, 21, 45, 72, 101, 110, 132, and 144:1-11. Up until recently, especially in the Wellhausen School, scholars have been prone to place these Royal Psalms, as well as the psalms in general, in the post-exilic period. In doing so, they presupposed that the one who is praised as "king" in these psalms is the community of Israel;[y] but the "king" is certainly to be understood as none other than an individual. Or, it was conjectured that some foreign king was intended, perhaps one of the Ptolemies who was favorably disposed to the Jews. But this, too, is untenable because the king in Psalms 2, 20, and 110 has his throne in Zion. A third possibility has been to try to make the psalms refer to one of the Maccabean priest-princes. However, the psalms we possess which actually do come from such later times, in the Apocrypha and in the so-called Psalms of Solomon, are feeble imitations of the ancient pattern or are so corroded by introspection [*Reflexion*] that they are sharply distinguishable from the vigorous and spirited Royal Psalms in the canon. To this must be added the fact that in these psalms the divinely inspired singer occasionally pronounces an oracle (Pss. 20:6 ff. [Heb., 20:7 ff.] 110:1 ff., 4 ff.); but prophecy in the Maccabean Period, as we are expressly told in I Maccabees 4:46, had ceased. Accordingly, the natural explanation, that the Royal Psalms belong to the royal period of ancient Israel, is to be affirmed. All arguments to the contrary are silenced when we compare the Babylonian and Egyptian poems and recognize the great similarity of the poetic forms.

---

[y] community of Israel, an allegorical explanation which is clearly mistaken, since the "king" in these Psalms is surely an individual.

---

[42] Cf. H. Gunkel, *Einleitung in die Psalmen*, secs. 5, 22; H. Gressman, *Der Messias* (Göttingen: Vandenhoeck & Ruprecht, 1929), index, under "Aegypten" and "Babel."

ᶻThe Israelite Royal Psalms, like the Royal Psalms in general, are to be classified according to the various situations for which they were sung. Psalm 20 was performed by the royal choir when the king went forth to battle. The royal Lament, Psalm 144:1-11 is to be assigned to the same setting. Psalm 18 is the thanksgiving prayer of a king upon his return from a campaign. Psalm 45 is a spirited and very ancient song sung to glorify the wedding of the sovereign. A song performed in the royal sanctuary on the occasion of the anniversary of the establishing of that sanctuary and of the founding of the kingdom is Psalm 132. Most frequent are those poems which were sung at the king's enthronement or at the annual royal festival (Pss. 2, 21, 72, and 110) ; on the day of his enthronement the king himself made a solemn vow (Ps. 101). There come to mind also the "Last Words of David" (II Sam. 23:1-7), the antiquity of which can hardly be questioned. On the other hand, the Lament of the pretender in verses 38, 46-51 (Heb., vss. 39, 47-52) of Psalm 89 belongs to the time after the fall of the state of Judah; standing in contrast to it are the verses that precede it, namely, verses 1 f., 5-18 (Heb., 2 f., 6-19), a hymn to Yahweh, and verses 3 f., 19-37 (Heb., 4 f., 20-38), a promise to David (cf. II Sam. 7).

Most of these psalms are full of enthusiastic praises of the king and exuberant good wishes for his welfare. Huge battle and victory scenes are invented in order to do him honor (as in Pss. 21:8 ff. [Heb., 21:9 ff.]; 45:3 ff. [Heb., 45:4 ff.]; and 110), the kind of scenes one finds portrayed in Babylonian and Egyptian art. In style some of these Royal Psalms conform to other psalm types. Thus, Psalms 144:1-11 and 89:46-51 (Heb., 89:47-52) belong to the Laments of the Individual, while Psalm 18 is one of the Thanksgiving Songs of the Individual. We find the same juxtaposition of songs of the prince and of the private citizen in Babylonia. For the origin of this literary type we must look, just as in Babylonia, to the area of the Royal Psalms.

ᶻ To the Royal Psalms (20; 21; 45; 72; 110) one may also add the following: Psalm 18, the thanksgiving prayer of a king; Psalm 101, the vow of a sovereign; Psalm 132, a song sung in the royal sanctuary in celebration of the occasion when the ark was brought to Zion; perhaps also Psalm 60, a Public Lament (vss. 1-5 [Heb., vss. 3-7]) to which has been added an oracle (vss. 6-8 [Heb., vss. 8-10]) and a Lament of the Israelite sovereign (vss. 9-12 [Heb., vss. 11-14]). There come to mind also the "Last Words of David" (II Sam. 23:1-7), the authenticity of which will not be questioned if one is acquainted with the Babylonian parallels (cf., e.g., Hehn, *Hymnen und Gebete an Marduk* ("Beiträge zur Assyriologie," 5), p. 212). [In *RGG*¹ the paragraph ends here.]

H. Conclusions about Liturgical Poetry

From what has been said above, it follows that the oldest religious poetry of Israel was part of its worship and that it existed in a great variety of forms. This cultic poetry was surely cultivated in the same circles in which the cult itself was nourished, that is, among the priests. Therefore, these lyrics might be called priestly poetry. The priests learned such poems by heart from earliest childhood, and they understood how to employ them in the correct manner. However, singers were also attached to the sanctuary, especially in later times; they performed these songs and were entrusted with their cultivation.[a] But in every case these songs existed in much the same way as did the songs of the people, that is, not written down at first but preserved in the memory.

The origin of this kind of poetry goes back to Israel's earliest period. This follows, in the first place, from the nature of the case: Israel's cultic poetry is as old as the cult itself.[b] The same conclusion follows from a comparison with Babylonian songs, which in their origin antedate Israel's history. This conclusion is confirmed by allusions in the historical and prophetical books: the Hymn is already attested by the time of Isaiah (6:3), and even earlier in the Song of Deborah and the Song of Miriam.[43] The existence of Laments of the Individual and Thanksgiving Songs is presupposed in Jeremiah, and Hosea composed poems in the style of the Community Lament.[c] What has been said here is true, in the first place, only of this type of poetry; nevertheless, some of the extant psalms may also be very old; for example, among the Hymns, Psalms 19:1-6 (Heb., 19:2-7); 29; 89:1 f., 5-18 (Heb., 89:2 f., 6-19).[d] In any case, the view which is very widespread at present, that psalm poetry as such originated in the time of the Babylonian Exile, in no way accords with the facts.[44]

[a] [This sentence is not in *RGG*[1].]
[b] cult itself, and the whole genre is by nature as primordial as the folk song, the folk saga, the legal verdict, and all other spiritual treasures of primitive folk life. The same conclusion
[c] the Public Lament.
[d] 6-19). In the latter, "Tabor and Hermon" are named as the places where Yahweh's name is praised: "Tabor and Hermon joyously praise thy name" (89:12 [Heb., 89:13]); cf. the example in Hehn, *Hymnen und Gebete an Marduk*, p. 313: "Let Babylon shout to thee with joy, let Esagila rejoice in thee!"

[43] "Deborahed" (Gunkel), *RGG*[2] 1, col. 1800. The Song of Miriam is treated in the article "Mirjam" (see n. 22 above).
[44] "Psalterbuch," 2 (see n. 1 above), col. 1629; cf. also chap. 4 below.

4

NON-LITURGICAL PSALMS OR
"SPIRITUAL SONGS"

VERY many[e] of the psalms which have come down to us do not
belong to the poetry of the cult. They presuppose no particular cultic
acts. They were not intended to be sung only on specific occasions but
could be sung or prayed anywhere. Accordingly, out of the Cult Songs
have grown Spiritual Poems. Here a kind of piety which has freed
itself of all ceremonies expresses itself, a religion of the heart.[f] Here
something wonderful has happened. Religion has cast off the shell of
sacred usage, in which, until now, it has been protected and nurtured:
it has come of age. These Spiritual Songs, as much as anything else in
the Old Testament, stand closest to the Gospel.[g] The spiritual and in-
tellectual current which manifests itself in these Psalms is closely related to that of the prophets; for prominent in the latter, too, is a spirit
which disdains sacrifice and ceremonies. Prophets and these psalmists
are unanimous in stating what Yahweh does not want: he does *not*
want sacrifice (Ps. 50 is an example).[45] But prophet and psalmist differ
in what they affirm. According to the great prophets, it is primarily
morality that is required; according to these psalmists, it is a sincere

e Most of the psalms which have
f heart. Indeed, even the worshiping congregation has vanished from many of
these Psalms; the soul stands alone before its God. Here something wonderful
g Gospel. The Christian community in every age has perceived this, and to
this day the Psalms are frequently included in editions of the New Testament.
The spiritual and

45 [Examples from the prophets: Amos 5:21-24; Hos. 6:6; 8:13; Mic. 6:6-8;
Isa. 1:12 ff.]

song (Ps. 50:14). But in both it is man's heart, his trust, and true piety which is called for.

Accordingly, we may now venture to say at what point the Cult Songs acquired this additional dimension. Certainly it happened through the influence of the prophetic spirit. That the prophets influenced the psalmists we know from the fact that the latter took over much from prophetic models. For example, Psalm 1 is an imitation of Jeremiah 17:5-8; Psalm 50 is a proclamation of the divine will in the style of the prophets; and the Eschatalogical Hymns,[46] especially, are imitations of a prophetic literary type. On the other hand, the prophets learned some things from the psalmists.[47] Now, we know from our sources that the first great literary prophets appeared in the eighth century. In the seventh century,[h] in the book of Deuteronomy, we see a clear literary descendant of these prophets. And it is in this century, i.e., still prior to the collapse of the state of Judah, that we can place—without being too rash—the origin of authentic "spiritual" poetry. Arguing in favor of this date is the fact that certain psalms (28:8; 61:6-7 [Heb., 61: 7-8]; 63:11 [Heb., 63:12]; 84:9 [Heb., 84:10]; I Sam. 2:10) close with a prayer for the reigning king. These prayers, which were doubtless added later when the psalms were to be performed in the royal temple in Jerusalem, certainly stem from the royal period. However, they do not differ substantially from others of the same literary type. Thus, we conclude from such a comparison that the style already existed as an established literary form in the royal period and that the Exile did not signify a turning point—at least not a significant turning point —in the history of psalm poetry.

The same conclusion follows from a psalm such as chapter 3 of Lamentations,[48] which, judging from its inclusion in that book, was written during the Exile, and also from Psalm 18, a Thanksgiving Song composed for a king; both poems are, in their whole atmosphere, totally derivative. Our position is also supported by the conformity of the "Laments[i] of Jeremiah"[49] to the biblical Laments, for Jeremiah

[h] In the seventh century, in the book of Deuteronomy, the work of prophetic epigons is clearly discernible. And it is in this century
[i] the "Monologues" of Jeremiah

[46] Cf. below, chap. 5, sec. A.
[47] Cf. above, chap. 1, and "Propheten," IIB, 3m (Gunkel), *RGG²* 4, cols. 1552 ff.
[48] "Klagelieder Jeremiae" (see n. 28 above).
[49] ["*Klagegedichte Jeremias*," the "confessions" or "psalms" of Jeremiah; see p. v of the book cited in the next footnote.]

was certainly not the originator of this literary type! Literary types are never invented by an individual writer; rather, they develop slowly and gradually through the collaboration of whole generations. If anything, the literary forms employed by the great prophet in writing these poems show that he has been the borrower; for he speaks of his "pain" and of his "healing" metaphorically (Jer. 15:18 and 17:14), while the psalmists speak of them in a real sense.[50] Therefore, it must be supposed that Spiritual Laments were already in existence in his day.

It was in the post-exilic period, however, that this kind of psalm poetry was especially popular. It was here that genuine religion took refuge in a time when religion was beginning to show signs of ossification. It was here that the prophetic ideas lived on and continued to exert an influence. The resulting songs, often quite individualistic and subjective, were then performed in the temple[j] (in much the same way as the modern missionary tunes have been taken up into the hymnals of the church). In the cult these poems had their origin, and to the cult they finally returned. This retrograde process, however, must have set in very early, for already in the royal temple in Jerusalem such subjective songs as Psalms 28, 61, 63, 84, and I Samuel 2 were performed.

The two periods which saw the production of the religious lyric, and which we have set in contrast here, are,[k] to be sure, not to be separated from each other categorically, as if they had nothing to do with each other. The "spiritual" poetry gradually developed out of the cult poetry, and, on the whole, has preserved its literary forms. This explains the peculiar monotony of the Spiritual Songs; for having originated in the formularies of the cult they seldom abandoned completely the formal requirements [*das Formelhafte*] of cultic poetry. Furthermore, after the origin of spiritual poetry, cultic poetry continued to exist, and it is for this reason that not a few Cult Songs or portions of Cult Songs are found in the Psalter.[51] Moreover, some songs stand in closer relation to the cult than others. For instance, those types which were performed before the assembled cult community, such as the

---

[j] temple and, thus, transmitted to us as the hymnbook of the temple (in much
[k] are naturally not to be separated from each other in a mechanical way. The "spiritual" poetry

[50] Cf. W. Baumgartner, *Die Klagegedichte des Jeremias* ("Beihefte zur Zeitschrift für die alttestamentliche Wissenschaft," 32; Giessen: Töpelmann, 1917).

[51] Cf. above, chap. 2, and chap. 3, secs. A-F.

Community Laments and the Community Hymns,[1] have the older form in a purer state.[m] At the latest stage, on the contrary, stand those Laments of the Individual which were neither part of a specific rite nor intended for cultic performance but which the sick person composed on his bed of pain or with which the sufferer comforted himself. In these psalms only here and there does an image suggest the older form (an example is Ps. 51:7).

[1] such as the Public Laments and the Public Hymns, have the

[m] state. Admittedly, in these psalms cultic acts are more infrequent; nonetheless, most of these psalms were composed for performance in the temple, and can therefore be compared with our chorales. At the latest stage

CLASSIFICATION OF PSALMS
IN THE PSALTER

THE songs contained in the Psalter may now be divided into their main classes.

A. HYMNS

First, there are the Hymns. Here the relationship to the cult frequently still stands out clearly. Songs in praise of Yahweh were sung by the community at worship in every period, and even the forms of the Hymns have remained substantially the same as in former times. Just as Miriam sang, "Sing to the Lord, for he has triumphed gloriously," so one still hears in the Song of the Three Young Men: "Bless the Lord . . . for he has rescued us from Hades" (vs. 6b). We cannot but admire the tremendous persistence of form which survived throughout the entire history of Israel. The content of the Hymn remains Yahweh's majesty. Thus, in these songs we are confronted with the total power and majesty of the God of Israel; when viewed as poetry, these Hymns are probably the most precious in the Psalter. Mythology, which[n] from earliest times had found its way into the Hymns, lived on in these songs, although in subdued form.[52] Alongside, however, stands the glorification of the God who has revealed himself in the history of Israel. Legendary material appears in the Hymns, and many times—mostly not to the advantage of the poetic effect—fills them com-

[n] which from earliest times had filled the Hymns, lived on

[52] "Mythus," IIIA, 4 (Gunkel), RGG^2 4, cols. 385 ff.

pletely (two examples are Pss. 104 and 105). It is a mark of an individualistic age when the poet[o] gives expression in the Hymn to his innermost experiences, or, standing alone under the starry heavens, contemplates the greatness of God and the smallness of man (Ps. 8).

Prophetic influence has many times left its imprint on the Hymns, for example, in the lovely Psalm 103, but more especially in a characteristic variety of Hymns, the Eschatological Hymns. The prophets, looking retrospectively in spirit to a great turning point, which [to them] had already taken place, composed the hymn of jubilation which the final generation would one day sing.[53] This marvelous literary form, which never fails to make an impact, the psalmists had learned from the prophets. Thus, the lyric poetry which the prophets had learned from the psalmists is given back to them in a new form.[p] These Eschatological Hymns in the Psalms, which have often been misinterpreted by commentators and made to refer to this or that historical event, sing of the end-time, when the nations will assemble in tumult and the mountains will fall into the heart of the seas—until the city of God, wonderfully transformed into a paradise, appears, and Yahweh with one final mighty blow brings all wars to an end (Ps. 46; another example is Ps. 149). Such Eschatological Hymns were still being composed in the latest period of the Old Testament and are even found in the New ("Glory to God in the highest," Luke 2:14; also Luke 1:46 ff.; 1:68 ff.; Rev. 11:17 ff.; 19:1 f.; 19:6 ff.). Closely related to these Eschatological Hymns of the psalmists are the latter's pronouncements concerning the future, which likewise imitate the style of the prophets (Pss. 82; 85:1-4, 8-13 [Heb., 85:2-5, 9-14]; 126:1-3) and are heard even in the latest Old Testament period (Tob. 13:9 ff.; Ps. Sol. 11[q]). [54]

---

[o] the poet sings in his own name and, standing alone under

[p] form. Here especially we become aware of a reciprocal relation between prophets and psalmists. That precisely these two groups so strongly influenced each other is explained by their inherent relationship: the psalmists, too, by reason of their divine inspiration, had the right to proclaim oracles. These Eschatological Hymns

[q] Ps. Sol. 11). Just how ancient this type of Hymn is, is shown by Psalm 2, where an eschatological song of this kind is sung in honor of a (reigning) king of Zion.

---

[53] "Propheten," IIB, 3m (see n. 47 above).

[54] Cf. H. Gunkel, *Einleitung in die Psalmen*, sec. 9.

B. COMMUNITY LAMENTS

A second major class is constituted by the Community Laments.[r] Examples are Psalms 44, 74, 79, 80, 83, and 89:38 ff. Here is the place where the woeful plight of the people is depicted; it is bewailed and lamented with copious tears. These are the vengeful cries of a tormented people, affronted in that which they consider most holy.

The content of these Laments may be divided into three parts. First, there is the lament proper, the purpose of which is to move Yahweh to compassion, and in which the complaint about the mockery of the enemy plays a special role, for to the Jews the scorn of the surrounding peoples was piercing to the soul. Then comes the prayer to Yahweh to remove the calamity, whatever it may be. At this point all kinds of arguments are put before Yahweh with the intent of moving him to think graciously upon his people and intervene in their behalf. Here belong especially the reminders of their close relationship with Yahweh, which he should not forget, or the memory of the past, in which he has so often helped them. Finally, there is the certainty of a hearing.[55]

The precise dating of these psalms is very difficult or even impossible to determine, even in cases where they refer to definite events. For these poems represent liturgical formulas more than they do poems written for the occasion. Moreover, the century from the time of Ezra's giving of the Law until the coming of Alexander the Great is an almost unknown quantity.

C. THANKSGIVING SONGS OF THE INDIVIDUAL

Among the Thanksgiving Songs of the Individual[s] are a few which clearly presuppose the worship service and which were to be sung at the thank offering.[56] Others expressly reject the thank offering. Thus, we have here a struggle, closely related to that waged by the prophets, against the institution of sacrifice:

> I will praise the name of God with a song;
> I will magnify him with thanksgiving.
> This will please the Lord more than an ox
> or a bull with horns and hoofs.
> (Ps. 69:30-31 [Heb., 69:31-32])

[r] the Public Laments.
[s] Among the Private Thanksgiving Songs are a few

[55] Cf. above, chap. 3, sec. B.
[56] For examples, see above, chap. 3, sec. D.

A similar example is Psalm 40:6 (Heb., 40:7). In form, however, the Spiritual Thanksgiving Songs are scarcely distinguishable from that of the Thank Offering Songs.

D. SPIRITUAL LAMENTS OF THE INDIVIDUAL

The Spiritual Laments of the Individual constitute the largest group of songs in the Psalter. Here, and in the Wisdom Literature, is the place where individuality is expressed in the Old Testament. These songs, above all, are the prototypes of Protestant hymnody. From the standpoint of poetry, they are not always outstanding; but from the standpoint of religion, they are the imperishable treasure in the Psalter. At first, one might think it strange that precisely in such laments— songs of sighing, weeping, and rending of the heart[t]—the personal life stands out so strongly, until one realizes that here too the rule applies that grievous woes give release to the life of the spirit. Pure and authentic religion is to be found only where tremendous struggles have been experienced.[u] The man whose ways are prospering can perhaps do without the divine helper; but the sufferer, who despairs of humanity and of the world, will lift up his hands, out of the depths of his distress, to the God who dwells on high.

But how is it that there were at that time so many sufferers that their prayers constitute the material of a special literary type in the Psalter? The answer to this we learn from the descriptions which the psalmists themselves paint: they speak of themselves as the poor, the distressed, the humble, and the silent faithful. They complain of oppression by the rich, the mighty, the proud, and the insolent. Everywhere it is assumed that these poor very frequently are identical with the pious, while most of the evildoers care nothing about God. Thus the poor and the rich stand opposed to each other, not only as two social strata but, at the same time, as two religious groups. We know that such conditions existed during early Christian times, as well as during the Greek period, when the nobles and the wealthy identified with the Hellenistic rulers and Hellenistic culture, while humble folk remained true to the old religion. The same was doubtless true in the Persian period, when Ezra and Nehemiah had to battle against mixed marriages and betrayal of the fatherland—by the nobles and the high priests!

---

[t] heart—the individual has won the right to give expression to his personal experiences; it may seem strange that songs originally connected with sickness are the place where the personal life stands out

[u] experienced; distress leads to God. The man whose

Just how old this problem is we learn from the book of Jeremiah, where the prophet not only sings Laments himself but identifies himself as one of the "poor"; thus, in Jeremiah 20:13:

> Sing to the Lord:
>> praise the Lord!
> For he has delivered the life of the needy[57]
>> from the hand of evildoers.

Conditions such as these, which began to develop even prior to the fall of the [Israelite and Judahite] states and have been a part of Judaism throughout its whole history, form the background for the understanding of these Laments. The perennial misery of life—this explains why precisely this literary type has had such an appeal for people.

Remnants of the old style are found (1) in the presupposition of sickness (now understood only in a figurative sense, as in Jeremiah), (2) in ideas borrowed from the expiation rites, and (3) in the certainty of a hearing.[58] In outline such Laments of the Individual are closely related to the Community Laments, and in later times the two are occasionally fused (an example is Ps. 94).

The principal components of this type must be described. First, the lament proper depicts the suffering of the poet, with the purpose of moving Yahweh to compassion. In doing so, however, the poet also brings relief to his burdened heart. Such laments are extraordinarily emotional. The singer is especially fond of saying that he has already descended to the underworld: the waters of Sheol [*Hades*] have swallowed him up (Pss. 69:1 f. [Heb., 69:2 f.]; 88:3 f. [Heb., 88:4 f.]); thus, we have here a picture similar to that in the Thanksgiving Songs.[59] Especially frequent are the psalmist's complaints about his enemies, who deride him in his misery and lie in wait for his death. These are those "others," the prosperous children of the world, who constitute a group standing in opposition to the pious and hope to live to see the foolishness of their faith.[60] Now and then the poet complains about his separation from Zion (an example is Ps. 42). Here is an indication that even this very personal piety cannot dispense entirely with visible symbols. Here and there, and especially at the end of the song, the

---

[57] [Gunkel's rendering: "the soul of the poor."]
[58] Cf. above, chap. 3, sec. E.
[59] Cf. above, chap. 3, sec. D.
[60] "Vergeltung," II (im AT), 1-8 (Gunkel), *RGG*[2] 5, cols. 1529-33 (esp. II, 4, col. 1532).

horizon is enlarged: the suppliant remembers his people and the common need. In such passages personal poems may become corporate ones (examples are Pss. 130:7 and 131:3). Many times in this type of lament the psalmists struck the primal notes of piety, unsurpassed in their tenderness and depth (cf., e.g., Ps. 42).

Then there is the entreaty, which corresponds to the lament and[v] sometimes alternates with it. Frequently we find an entreaty for revenge on one's enemies; out of such entreaties, perhaps in imitation of older, cultic curses, the genre of Imprecatory Psalms developed (an example is Ps. 109). The suppliant appended all kinds of arguments, which he put before God in the hope of moving him to consider his cause. For prayer in antiquity was more childlike and, at the same time, more calculating than our own. One expressed those thoughts which God should consider. Here belong, above all, the expressions of confidence that God will surely help (cf., e.g., Pss. 3:3 ff. [Heb., 3:4 ff.] and 22:9 f. [Heb., 22:10 f.]). For to just such expressions of confidence God will give heed—such was the hope of the suppliant, who believed that God could not let such confidence go begging. Often the beauty of these psalms consists in this moving alternation of passionate laments and entreaties, on the one hand, and confident hope on the other (e.g., Pss. 3, 123, 130). There are some psalms in which only this confidence is expressed, the laments and entreaties having receded into the background. In these Psalms of Confidence what was once simply a motif, a single idea, has become an independent vehicle of expression. Their serene and tender style is delightful (an example is Ps. 23). Especially beautiful are those psalms in which one finds a gentle antiphony in the depths of the soul (an example is Ps. 121). Frequently one finds all sorts of meditations in which the psalmist indulges in order to win confidence for himself or to win Yahweh to his side. Sometimes the poet reflects upon the long night of death and the brevity of human life (an example is Ps. 6:6 [Heb., 6:7]); or he reflects upon the basic rule of divine conduct, namely, the doctrine of retribution. Here is the point, therefore, at which lyric poetry intermingled with wisdom poetry, about which more will be said later.[61]

The two principal types of Lament Psalms are the Psalms of Innocence and the Penitential Psalms.

In the first type the poet asks, in passionate excitement, the reason

---

[v] and arbitrarily alternates with it; here, too, structure is not the strong point of Hebrew poetry. Frequently we find

[61] Cf. below, chap. 5, sec. E.

for his suffering, for he can find absolutely nothing in himself that would incur it. With strong protests he asserts his innocence and demands the recognition of his righteousness (examples are Pss. 17 and 26), a manner of speaking which is reflected in the poems in Jeremiah and especially in the majestic speeches of Job. The poet is then all the more violent in attacking his enemies; hence, alongside Psalms of Innocence one finds Imprecatory Psalms.

Very different from these are the Penitential Psalms, of which Psalm 51 is an example. Here the singer is convinced that it is because of his own sins that the wrath of God has descended upon him. Every thought which he presents is for the purpose of inducing God to think kindly of his sins. Thus, for example, he points to human sinfulness in general, in order to put his own sins in a better light.

Very commonly the Lament Psalm concludes with the certainty of a hearing. Many times this kind of conclusion represents such a noticeable change of tone that some have even thought a poem such as Psalm 22 should be divided into two parts. The psalm begins with lamentation and complaint and closes with rejoicing and jubilation. The same phenomenon occurs in the "Laments of Jeremiah."[w] Very frequently the psalmist adds to his prayer a vow to sing a Thanksgiving Psalm after his deliverance; sometimes he even voices the Thanksgiving Psalm in advance of the deliverance (Ps. 22 is a classic example). The same is frequently true of the Babylonian Laments.

E. MIXED TYPES AND FURTHER DEVELOPMENTS[x]

A little has already been said about some of the mixed types and the later development of the types discussed above. Mixtures or inner transformations occur with great frequency when the literature we are discussing becomes old, especially when the original setting of the literary types has been forgotten or is no longer clear.[62]

One such transformation is seen, for example, in the songs celebrating Yahweh's enthronement,[63] in which the characteristic expression is "Yahweh has become king" (an example is Ps. 97). Such

---

[w] the "Monologues" of Jeremiah.

[x] [The arrangement of the materials in this section differs considerably from *RGG*[1] to *RGG*[2], but the content is substantially the same.]

[62] "Literaturgeschichte, biblische," 2c (see n. 21 above), cols. 1678-79.

[63] [For Gunkel's views on the evidence for an enthronement festival of Yahweh, and for his assessment of Mowinckel's arguments regarding such a festival, see his *Einleitung in die Psalmen*, sec. 3, esp. pp. 100-16.]

psalms[y] praise Yahweh's dominion and are thus imitations of the Royal Psalms which were customarily sung at the enthronement of the earthly king but then, under prophetic influence, were transformed into songs heralding the coming dominion of Yahweh. Thus, in their final stages they constitute prophetic, eschatological poetry.

It is also an imitation of the prophetic style when the poet proclaims Torah, as Yahweh's prophets once did. Copying the form of the theophany as found in the prophets, he represents Yahweh as appearing in storm and fire (Ps. 50).

The following are mixed types. At the end of a Lament there may be a Thanksgiving Song, which the sufferer will sing once he has been delivered from his calamity (an example is Ps. 22:27 ff. [Heb., 22:28 ff.]). In much the same way the author of a Thanksgiving Song may cite a Lament Psalm which he had sung in former times (Isa. 38:10-14). The Thanksgiving Song can begin or conclude with a Hymn if the enthusiasm of the one giving thanks is so high-pitched that he cannot be content with only his personal thanks (Pss. 66 and 103). The Lament, as well, may contain hymnic motifs in order to assail God more effectively (Ps. 44:1-8 [Heb., 44:2-9]); or a Hymn may close with a prayer borrowed from the style of the Lament (Ps. 104:35).[z] Many other examples could be given.

[a]In addition, there is the enrichment which the psalm style experienced through the liturgy. It was a custom in worship to sing psalms antiphonally. The next step suggested itself: to join pieces from various literary types into a single unit.[b] An example is Psalm 60, where in the midst of a Community Lament spoken with reference to the ruler of Israel, a divine Oracle announcing victory is inserted (vss. 6-8 [Heb., vss. 8-10]). This combination of Community Lament and Oracle was seized upon by the prophets and elaborated into magnificent pictures (examples are Isa. 33:1-13; 26:8-21; Mic. 7:7 ff.). In the prophetic presentations the prayer of the community usually comes

[y] These psalms sing of Yahweh's future dominion and are thus prophetic-eschatological poems; but with them the psalmists blended imitations of the Royal Psalms which were customarily sung at the enthronement of the king. It is also an imitation of the prophetic

[z] 104:35). Both are very common in Babylonian literature. Many other examples

[a] The liturgy, especially, fostered the development of mixed types in the Psalms. It was a custom

[b] unit. Near the end of the period of psalm poetry such hybrids became increasingly common. An example of mixed style resulting from liturgical influence [*liturgische Stilmischung*] is Psalm 60

first and then the wonderful preview of the future. Here again the psalmists learned from the prophets and sang moving songs in which suffering and consolation stand wondrously side by side (Ps. 126). Thus in Psalm 85 the first part proclaims in triumphant, prophetic tones the deliverance that has been granted (vss. 1-3 [Heb., vss. 2-4]); then the community offers a yearning lament (vss. 4-7 [Heb., vss. 5-8]), while in the third part a prophetic voice takes over and again ascends to the heights, ending with a vision of the future (vss. 8-13 [Heb., vss. 9-14]). There is another kind of liturgy, in which, again, the mixture of the prophetic and the lyric appears: when the community marches into the sanctuary singing a Hymn (Ps. 95:1-7a), a powerful Diatribe in the style of the prophets[64] resounds in reply (vss. 7b-11).

The lyric poetry of later times, especially, was altered when it came to be filled increasingly with meditation. Thus there are psalms which do not once contain the form of a prayer but consist entirely of pious reflections. Such psalms sometimes proclaim the doctrine of retribution in the popular form of blessings for the righteous (examples are Pss. 1 and 128) or in the form of the exhortation (Ps. 37), in both cases following the pattern set in wisdom poetry. Ultimately, the pious grew uncertain of the doctrine of retribution,[65] and they underwent a tremendous struggle in order to gain reassurance that the doctrine still held. Thus, poems were written which have affinities with the book of Job,[66] although they are inferior to it in quality. The author of Psalm 37 asserts the old belief in the face of all doubts in the style of the Warning. The writer of Psalm 73 recounts his inner struggles and ends with the wonderful words:

> Whom have I in heaven but thee?
>> And there is nothing upon earth that I desire besides thee.[67]
>>> (v. 25)

Psalm 32 offers a very odd combination of Thanksgiving Song and Wisdom Poem. The psalmist relates what God has done for him in the Thanksgiving Song, and for the benefit of the younger generation

---

[64] "Propheten," IIB, 3m (see n. 47 above).
[65] "Vergeltung," IIA (see above, n. 60), esp. sec. 5 (col. 1532).
[66] "Hiobbuch" (see n. 6 above).
[67] [Gunkel's rendering:
If I have only thee,
I shall ask for neither heaven nor earth.]

joins to it his teaching and admonition. cUltimately, such meditations permeated and undermined the lyric, as can be seen most clearly in the post-canonical Psalms of Solomon.

At the end the literary types decay more and more. For example, in some of the acrostic poems the poet seems to move about among the various types quite chaotically as he proceeds down the alphabetical scale (Lam. 3 is an example).[68] The poems of the latest period, especially those of Sirach, move about on an undisciplined course until, finally, psalm poetry gradually dies out.

c Such meditations came to permeate the lyric, as can be seen in the great acrostic psalm, Psalm 119, and especially in the post-canonical Psalms of Solomon.

[68] "Klagelieder Jeremiae," 3 (see n. 28 above), col. 1051.

List of Literary Types
and Technical Terms

Certainty of a hearing (*Gewissheit der Erhörung*)

Community Hymns (*Hymnen der Gemeinde*)

Community Lament(s) (*Volksklagelied, Volksklagepsalm, Klagelieder der Gemeinde*)

Confession of Innocence of the Community (*Unschuldsbekenntnis des Volkes*)

Cult Song (*Kultuslied*)

Diatribe (*Scheltrede*)

Eschatological Hymns (*eschatologische Hymnen*)

Funeral Dirges (*Leichenlieder*)

Hymn (*Hymnus*)

Hymn of the Seraphim (*Hymnus der Seraphim*)

Incantation (*Zauberwort*)

Imprecatory Psalms (*Rachepsalmen*)

Lament (*Klagelied*)

Laments of the Individual (*Klagelieder des Einzelnen*)

Lament Psalms (*Klagepsalmen*)

Literary forms (*Formensprache*)

Literary type, type, genre (*Gattung*)

Liturgy of Entrance (*Einzugs-Tora*)

Oracle (*Orakel*)

Pentitential Prayer of the Community (*Bussgebet des Volkes*)

Pentitential Psalms (*Busspsalmen*)

Pilgrim Song (*Wallfahrtslied*)

Prophetic Saying (*Prophetenspruch*)

Psalms of Confidence (*Vertrauenspsalmen*)

Psalms of Innocence (*Unschuldspsalmen*)

Royal Psalms (*Königspsalmen, Königslieder*)

Setting in life (*Sitz im Leben*)

Songs of the Individual (*Lieder des Einzelnen*)

Spiritual Laments (*geistliche Klagelieder*)

Spiritual Poems (*geistliche Gedichte*)

Spiritual Laments of the Individual (*geistliche Klagelieder des Einzelnen*)

Spiritual Songs (*geistliche Lieder*)

Spiritual Thanksgiving Songs (*geistliche Danklieder*)

Thank Offering Song (*Dankopferlied*)

Thanksgiving Psalm (*Dankpsalm*)

Thanksgiving Songs (*Danklieder*)

Thanksgiving Songs of the Individual (*Danklieder des Einzelnen*)

Torah Interrogation (*Tora-Frage*)

Warning (*Mahnrede*)

Wisdom poetry (*Weisheitsdichtung*)

Work Song (*Arbeitslied*)

For Further Reading

By Hermann Gunkel:

A bibliography of Gunkel's works down to 1922 appears in the Festschrift presented to him entitled ΕΥΧΑΡΙΣΤΗΡΙΟΝ. *Studien zur Religion und Literatur des Alten und Neuen Testaments Hermann Gunkel zum 60. Geburtstage, dem 23. Mai 1922 dargebracht . . .* , edited by Hans Schmidt. 1. Teil, *Zur Religion und Literatur des Alten Testaments;* 2. Teil, *Zur Religion und Literatur des Neuen Testaments* ("Forschungen zur Religion und Literatur des Alten und Neuen Testaments," N.F. 19, 1 and 2 [Göttingen: Vandenhoeck & Ruprecht, 1923]). Vol. 2, pp. 214-25.

Additional titles since 1922 are listed by L. Hennequin, in *Dictionnaire de la Bible* (Paris: Letouzey & Ané). Supplement 3 (1938), 1374–77.

Gunkel's early work, beginning with *Die Wirkung des heiligen Geistes* (1888), was in the area of New Testament studies, and included a commentary on I Peter in the series edited by Johannes Weiss, "Die Schriften des Neuen Testaments" (1st ed., 1906; 2nd ed., 1908; 3rd ed., 1917). His monograph on the history-of-religions approach to the New Testament, *Zum religionsgeschichtlichen Verständnis des Neuen Testaments* ("Forschungen zur Religion und Literatur des Alten und Neuen Testaments," 1 [Göttingen: Vandenhoeck & Ruprecht, 1903; reissued, 1910, 1930]) was translated into English in *The Monist* (Chicago: Open Court Publishing Company), No. 3 (April, 1903), pp. 398 ff.

Cf. Werner Klatt, *Hermann Gunkel: zu seiner Theologie der Religionsgeschichte und zur Entstehung der formgeschichtlichen Methode* ("Forschungen zur Religion und Literatur des Alten und Neuen Testaments," 100; Göttingen: Vandenhoeck & Ruprecht, 1969). An analysis of Gunkel's work, based on a Hamburg dissertation in 1966; cf. *Journal of Biblical Literature,* 88 (1969), pp. 508 f. Klatt's article, "Die 'Eigentümlichkeit' der israelitischen Religion in der Sicht von Hermann Gunkel," *Evangelische Theologie*, 28 (1968), pp. 153–60, discusses Gunkel's position on the so-called peculiarity of the religion of Israel, in light of Otto Dibelius's comment, from his student days, that "Gunkel was certainly not the kind of interpreter of the Old Testament that a Christian theology student would wish for. . . . That the Old Testament was in any way a revelation of God to man was not something one learned from Gunkel" (*In the Service of the Lord: The Autobiography of Bishop Otto Dibelius* [New York: Holt, Rinehart & Winston, 1964], p. 46).

For Further Reading

IN ENGLISH TRANSLATION

The Legends of Genesis. Translation, by W. S. Carruth, of *Die Sagen der Genesis* (1901). Chicago: Open Court Press, 1901. Reprinted as *The Legends of Genesis: The Biblical Saga and History,* with an introduction by W. F. Albright. New York: Schocken Books, 1964.

Interpretations, in *Biblical World,* 21 (1903), of Ps. 46 (pp. 28-31), Ps. 1 (pp. 120-23), Ps. 8 (pp. 206-09), Ps. 19 (pp. 281-83), Ps. 24 (pp. 366-70), Ps. 42 (pp. 433-39); in *Biblical World,* 22 (1904), of Ps. 103 (pp. 209-15), Ps. 137 (pp. 290-93), Ps. 149 (pp. 363-66).

Israel and Babylon. Translated by E. S. B. Philadelphia: J. J. McVey, 1904.

The History of Religion and Old Testament Criticism. London: Williams & Norgate. An address delivered at the fifth Weltkongress für freies Christentum and religiösen Fortschritt, 1910.

"The Poetry of the Psalms: Its Literary History and Its Application to the Dating of the Psalms," in *Old Testament Essays.* Edited by D. C. Simpson. London: Griffin, 1927. Pp. 118-42.

What Remains of the Old Testament and Other Essays. Translated by A. K. Dallas. Preface by James Moffatt. New York: Macmillan, 1928. Five essays are included:

> "What Is Left of the Old Testament?" (originally in *Die Deutsche Rundschau,* 41 [1914]);
>
> "Fundamental Problems of Hebrew Literary History" (*Deutsche Literaturzeitung,* 27 [1906], cols. 1797-1800, 1861-66);
>
> "The Religion of the Psalms" (*Die Christliche Welt,* 36 [1922], nos. 1, 2, 5, 6, 7);
>
> "The Close of Micah: A Prophetical Liturgy" (*Zeitschrift für Semitistik,* 2 [1924], pp. 145 ff.);
>
> "Jacob" (*Preussische Jahrbücher,* 176 [June, 1919]).

COMMENTARIES

Genesis übersetzt und erklärt. ("Göttinger Handkommentar zum Alten Testament," I/1.) Göttingen: Vandenhoeck & Ruprecht, 1901; 5th ed., 1922; 7th ed., 1965. Contains a personal sketch of Gunkel's academic career and his development as a scholar, by Walter Baumgartner.

Ausgewählte Psalmen. Göttingen: Vandenhoeck & Ruprecht, 1904; 4th rev. ed., 1917.

Die Psalmen übersetzt und erklärt. ("Göttinger Handkommentar zum Alten Testament," II/2) Göttingen: Vandenhoeck & Ruprecht; 4th ed., 1926.

Einleitung in die Psalmen: Die Gattungen der religösen Lyrik Israels. Completed by Joachim Begrich. ("Göttinger Handkommentar, Ergänzungsband zur II. Abteilung.") Göttingen: Vandenhoeck & Ruprecht, 1933; reissued 1966.

Der Prophet Esra (IV. Esra). Tübingen: J. C. B. Mohr, 1900.

Die Propheten. Göttingen: Vandenhoeck & Ruprecht, 1917.

The Psalms

MONOGRAPHS, ARTICLES

"Die israelitische Literatur," in *Die Kultur der Gegenwart,* I/7. Berlin and
Leipzig: B. G. Teubner. Vol. 1 (1906), pp. 51-102.

*Schöpfung und Chaos in Urzeit und Endzeit: eine religionsgeschichtliche
Untersuchung uber Gen. 1 und Ap. Joh. 12.* Göttingen: Vandenhoeck &
Ruprecht, 1895; reissued, 1921.

Reden und Aufsätze. Göttingen: Vandenhoeck & Ruprecht, 1913.

Gunkel served as an editor for the series "Forschungen zur Religion und
Literatur des Alten und Neuen Testaments" and also for both the first
and second editions of *Die Religion in Geschichte und Gegenwart.* For
RGG² (1927-31) he was editor-in-chief along with Leopold Zscharnack
and contributed over a hundred articles himself.

On the Psalms:

RECENT SURVEYS

BENTZEN, AAGE. *Introduction to the Old Testament.* Copenhagen: Gad,
1948. Vol. 1, pp. 119-202 ("Poetry").

JOHNSON, A. R. "The Psalms," in *The Old Testament and Modern Study:
A Generation of Discovery and Research.* Edited by H. H. Rowley.
Oxford: Clarendon, 1951. Pp. 162-209.

GALLING, KURT. "Psalmen, I. Im AT," in *Die Religion in Geschichte und
Gegenwart.* 3rd ed. Tübingen: J. C. B. Mohr. Vol. 5 (1961), cols. 672-84.

ANDERSON, G. W. "The Psalms," in *Peake's Commentary on the Bible.*
Edited by M. Black and H. H. Rowley. New York: Thomas Nelson,
1962. Pp. 409-43, especially 410 f. (section 359b hails Gunkel as "the
pioneer" in form criticism of the Psalms).

HEMPEL, J. "Psalms, Book of," in *The Interpreter's Dictionary of the
Bible.* Edited by G. A. Buttrick and others. New York and Nashville:
Abingdon, 1962. Vol. 3, pp. 942-58.

JOHNSON, A. R. "Psalms," in *Dictionary of the Bible.* Edited by James
Hastings, rev. ed. by F. C. Grant and H. H. Rowley. New York: Scribner's, 1963. Pp. 814-20, especially pp. 817 f. on Gunkel's work of
classification.

EISSFELDT, OTTO. *The Old Testament: An Introduction.* Translated from
the 3rd German ed. by Peter R. Ackroyd. New York: Harper & Row,
1965. Pp. 102-24 ("Cultic songs") and pp. 444-54 ("The Psalms").

MURPHY, ROLAND E., O. Carm. "Psalms," in *The Jerome Biblical Commentary.* Edited by Raymond E. Brown, Joseph A. Fitzmyer, and Roland
E. Murphy. Englewood Cliffs: Prentice-Hall, 1968. Art. 35, especially
35:6–17, pp. 570–75.

SUELZER, ALEXA, O.P. "Modern Old Testament Criticism," *ibid.,* Art. 70,
especially 70:29, 37–48, pp. 597–601.

KOCH, KLAUS. *The Growth of the Biblical Tradition: The Form-Critical
Method.* Translated from the second German edition by S. M. Cupitt.

44

New York: Scribner's, 1968. Especially pp. 3–4, 14, 24–25, 91–100, 159–82, though throughout it is Gunkel who looms as "the most venerable father" and "real pioneer" of form criticism.

SELLIN-FOHRER. *Introduction to the Old Testament.* Initiated by Ernst Sellin, completely revised and rewritten by Georg Fohrer. Translated by David E. Green. New York and Nashville: Abingdon, 1968. Especially sections 38–43, pp. 256 ff.

ON THE HISTORY OF RESEARCH

BLACKMAN, A. M. "The Psalms in Light of Egyptian Research," in *The Psalmists.* Edited by D. C. Simpson. Oxford: University Press, 1926. Pp. 177-97.

DRIVER, G. R. "The Psalms in Light of Babylonian Research," *ibid.* Pp. 109-75.

GRESSMANN, H. "The Development of Hebrew Psalmody," *ibid.* Pp. 1-21.

HALLER, MAX. "Ein Jahrzehnt Psalmforschung," *Theologische Rundschau,* N. F., 1 (1929), pp. 377-402.

MONTGOMERY, J. A. "Recent Developments in the Study of the Psalter," *Anglican Theological Review,* 16 (1934), pp. 185-98.

HEMPEL, J. "Neue Literatur zum Studium des Psalters," *Zeitschrift für die alttestamentliche Wissenschaft,* 56 (1938), pp. 171-74.

SELLERS, OVID R. "The Status and Prospects of Research concerning the Psalms," in *The Study of the Bible Today and Tomorrow.* Edited by Harold R. Willoughby. Chicago: University of Chicago Press, 1947. Pp. 129-43.

MOWINCKEL, SIGMUND. "Psalm Criticism between 1900 and 1935," *Vetus Testamentum,* 5 (1955), pp. 13-33, especially pp. 15 ff. on Gunkel and form criticism.

STAMM, J. J. "Ein Vierteljahrhundert Psalmenforschung," *Theologische Rundschau,* 23 (1955), pp. 1-68.

KAPELRUD, ARVID S. "Scandinavian Research in the Psalms after Mowinckel," *Annual of the Swedish Theological Institute* (Jerusalem). Edited by H. Kosmala and others. Vol. 4 (1965), pp. 74-90.

———. "Die skandinavische Einleitungswissenschaft zu den Psalmen," *Verkündigung und Forschung,* 11 (1966), pp. 62-93.

AP-THOMAS, D. R. "An Appreciation of Sigmund Mowinckel's Contribution to Biblical Studies," *Journal of Biblical Literature,* 85 (1966), pp. 315-25.

CLINES, D. J. A. "Psalm Research since 1955: I. The Psalms and the Cult," *Tyndale Bulletin,* 18 (1967), pp. 103–26. "II. The Literary Genres," *ibid.,* 20 (1969), pp. 105–25.

COMMENTARIES OF A TECHNICAL NATURE

BRIGGS, C. A. AND E. G. *A Critical and Exegetical Commentary on the Book of Psalms.* ("International Critical Commentary.") 2 vols. Edinburgh: T. & T. Clark, 1906-07; reprinted 1951-52.

BARNES, W. E. *The Psalms, with Introduction and Notes.* ("Westminster Commentaries.") 2 vols. London: Methuen, 1931.

SCHMIDT, HANS. *Die Psalmen.* ("Handbuch zum Alten Testament," I, 15.) Tübingen: J. C. B. Mohr, 1934.

BUTTENWIESER, MOSES. *The Psalms, Chronologically Treated with a New Translation.* Chicago: University of Chicago Press, 1938.

JAMES, FLEMING. *Thirty Psalmists: A Study in Personalities of the Psalter as Seen Against the Background of Gunkel's Type-Study of the Psalms.* New York: G. P. Putnam's Sons, 1938.

OESTERLEY, W. O. E. *The Psalms.* 2 vols. New York: Macmillan, 1939; 4th ed., 1953.

LESLIE, ELMER A. *The Psalms: Translated and Interpreted in the Light of Hebrew Life and Worship.* Nashville: Abingdon-Cokesbury Press, 1949.

KISSANE, EDWARD J. *The Book of Psalms: Translated from a Critically Revised Hebrew Text.* 2 vols. Dublin: Browne & Nolan, 1953-54.

McCULLOUGH, W. S., ET AL. "The Book of Psalms: Introduction and Exegesis," in *The Interpreter's Bible.* New York and Nashville: Abingdon, 1951–57. Vol. 4 (1955), pp. 1-763, especially pp. 6-7 (Gunkel "proposed a classification which has met with a wider acceptance than that of any other modern scholar," p. 6).

KRAUS, HANS-JOACHIM. *Psalmen.* ("Biblischer Kommentar," 15.) 2 vols. Neukirchen: Neukirchener Verlag, 1960; 2nd ed., 1962.

WEISER, ARTUR. *The Psalms.* "The Old Testament Library." Translated by Herbert Hartwell from the 5th rev. ed. of *Die Psalmen.* ("Das Alte Testament Deutsch," 14/15; 1959). Philadelphia: Westminster, 1962.

DAHOOD, MITCHELL, S. J. *Psalms I: 1-50: Introduction, Translation, and Notes. Psalms II: 51-100.* ("Anchor Bible," 16, 17.) Garden City: Doubleday, 1966 and 1968. A third volume is to follow.

DEISSLER, ALPHONSE. *Le livre des Psaumes.* ("Verbum Salutis, Ancien Testament," 1.) Paris: Beauchesne, 1966.

BECKER, JOACHIM. *Israel deutet seine Psalmen: Urform und Neuinterpretation in den Psalmen.* Stuttgarter Bibelstudien, 18. Stuttgart: Verlag Katholisches Bibelwerk, 1966.

SABOURIN, LEOPOLD, S.J. *The Psalms: Their Origin and Meaning.* Staten Island, New York: Alba House, 1969. 2 vols. Vol. 1, pp. 29–34, discusses Gunkel's method. The various categories are treated in vol. 1, pp. 179 ff., and in vol. 2.

COMMENTARIES AND TREATMENTS FOR THE GENERAL READER

PETERS, JOHN P. *The Psalms as Liturgies.* New York: Macmillan, 1922.

WELCH, ADAM C. *The Psalter in Life, Worship and History.* Oxford: Clarendon, 1926.

OESTERLEY, W. O. E. *A Fresh Approach to the Psalms.* London: Ivor Nicholson, 1937.

ROBINSON, THEODORE H. *The Poetry of the Old Testament.* London: Duckworth, 1947.

PATERSON, JOHN. *The Praises of Israel: Studies Literary and Relegious in the Psalms.* New York: Scribner's, 1950.

TERRIEN, SAMUEL L. *The Psalms and Their Meaning for Today.* Indianapolis: Bobbs-Merrill Co., 1951.

GUNN, GEORGE S. *God in the Psalms.* Edinburgh: St. Andrew's Press, 1956.

————. *Singers of Israel.* ("Bible Guides.") New York and Nashville: Abingdon, 1963.

LEWIS, C. S. *Reflections on the Psalms.* New York: Harcourt, Brace & Co., 1958.

SCOTT, R. B. Y. *The Psalms as Christian Praise.* New York: Association Press, 1959.

RHODES, ARNOLD B. *The Book of Psalms.* ("Layman's Bible Commentaries.") Richmond: John Knox Press, 1960.

TAYLOR, CHARLES L. *Let the Psalms Speak.* New York: Seabury, 1961.

CHASE, MARY ELLEN. *The Psalms and the Common Reader.* New York: W. W. Norton, 1962.

LAMB, JOHN R. *The Psalms in Christian Worship.* London: Faith Press, 1962.

WESTERMANN, CLAUS. *A Thousand Years and a Day: Our Time in the Old Testament.* Translated by Stanley Rudman. Philadelphia: Fortress Press, 1962. Pp. 263-71.

RINGGREN, HELMER. *The Faith of the Psalmists.* Philadelphia: Fortress Press, 1963.

DRIJVERS, P. *The Psalms: Their Structure and Meaning.* New York: Herder & Herder, 1965.

BARTH, CHRISTOPH. *Introduction to the Psalms.* Translated by R. A. Wilson. New York: Scribner's, 1966.

GUTHRIE, HARVEY H. *Israel's Sacred Songs: A Study of Dominant Themes.* New York: Seabury, 1966.

SCAMMAN, JOHN H. *Living With the Psalms.* Valley Forge, Pa.: Judson Press, 1967.

BULLOUGH, SEBASTIAN, O.P. "The Psalms," in *A New Catholic Commentary on Holy Scripture*, ed. by R. G. Fuller (London: Thomas Nelson, 1969), sections 381–410.

The Psalms

TOOMBS, LAWRENCE E. "The Psalms," in *The Interpreter's One-Volume Commentary on the Bible*, ed. by Charles M. Laymon (New York & Nashville: Abingdon, 1971), pp. 253–303.

Monographs and Specialized Articles

COLLECTIONS OF NONBIBLICAL SOURCES

PRITCHARD, JAMES (ed.). *Ancient Near Eastern Texts Relating to the Old Testament.* Princeton: Princeton University Press, 2nd ed. 1955.

THOMAS, D. WINTON (ed.). *Documents from Old Testament Times.* New York: Thomas Nelson & Sons, 1958.

ADDITIONAL LITERATURE ON NONBIBLICAL PARALLELS

JIRKU, ANTON. "Kana'anäische Psalmenfragmente in der vorisraelitischen Zeit Palästinas und Syriens," *Journal of Biblical Literature,* 52 (1933), pp. 108-20.

CUMMING, C. *The Assyrian and the Hebrew Hymns of Praise.* ("Columbia University Oriental Series," 12.) New York, 1934.

WIDENGREN, GEO. *The Akkadian and Hebrew Psalms of Lamentation as Religious Documents.* Uppsala: Almqvist & Wiksell, 1937.

PATTON, J. H. *Canaanite Parallels in the Book of Psalms.* Baltimore: Johns Hopkins Press, 1944.

For Ugaritic parallels, see the commentary by Dahood in the "Anchor Bible" (1966), but note the caution urged with regard to some of Dahood's interpretations by reviewers such as D. A. Robertson, in the *Journal of Biblical Literature,* 85 (1966), pp. 484-86.

(See also under "Collections of Nonbiblical Sources" and the entries by Blackman and Driver under "On the History of Research" above.)

ON QUMRAN PSALMS

RINGGREN, HELMER. *The Faith of Qumran: Theology of the Dead Sea Scrolls.* Translated by Emilie T. Sander. Philadelphia: Fortress Press, 1963. Brief introduction and bibliography on 1QH, the scroll of Thanksgiving Hymns, pp. 13-17.

HOLM-NIELSEN, SVEND. "The Importance of Late Jewish Psalmody for the Understanding of Old Testament Psalmodic Tradition," *Studia Theologica,* 14 (1960), pp. 1-53.

SANDERS, J. A. *The Psalms Scroll of Qumrân Cave 11.* New York: Oxford University Press, 1965.

―――. *The Dead Sea Psalms Scroll.* Ithaca, N. Y.: Cornell University Press, 1967.

CULT AND PSALMS

KRAUS, HANS-JOACHIM. *Worship in Israel.* Translated by Geoffrey Buswell from the 2nd, expanded ed. of *Gottesdienst in Israel.* Richmond: John Knox Press, 1966.

MOWINCKEL, SIGMUND. *The Psalms in Israel's Worship.* Translated by D. R. Ap-Thomas from the Norwegian original of 1951. 2 vols. New York and Nashville: Abingdon, 1962.

SZÖRÉNYI, ANDREAS. *Psalmen und Kult im Alten Testament (Zur Formgeschichte der Psalmen).* Budapest: Sankt Stefans Gesellschaft, 1961.

KAPELRUD, ARVID S. "The Role of the Cult in Old Israel," in *The Bible in Modern Scholarship: Papers Read at the 100th Meeting of the Society of Biblical Literature. December 28-30, 1964.* Edited by J. P. Hyatt. New York and Nashville: Abingdon, 1965. Pp. 44-56, with responses by B. Vawter, C.M., and H. G. May.

CLASSIFICATION OF THE PSALMS

WESTERMANN, CLAUS. *The Praise of God in the Psalms.* Translated by Keith R. Crim. Richmond: John Knox Press, 1965.

MURPHY, ROLAND E. "A New Classification of Literary Forms in the Psalms," *Catholic Biblical Quarterly,* 21 (1959), pp. 83-87. (Murphy notes that Westermann's classification, in the book just mentioned, not only develops Gunkel's approach but also challenges it by stressing the attitudes of man toward God involved in psalms [praise, pleading], as well as cultic factors.)

ON "KINGSHIP" AND "ENTHRONEMENT"

ENGNELL, IVAN. *Studies in Divine Kingship in the Ancient Near East.* Uppsala: Almqvist & Wiksell, 1943.

FRANKFURT, HENRI. *Kingship and the Gods: A Study of Ancient Near Eastern Religion as the Integration of Society and Nature.* New York: Cambridge University Press, 1948.

KRAUS, HANS-JOACHIM. *Die Königsherrschaft Gottes im Alten Testament: Untersuchungen zu den Liedern von Jahwes Thronbesteigung.* Tübingen: J. C. B. Mohr, 1951.

WIDENGREN, GEO. *Sakrales Königtum im Alten Testament und im Judentum.* ("Franz Delitzsch lecture for 1952.") Stuttgart: Kohlhammer, 1955.

JOHNSON, A. R. *Sacral Kingship in Ancient Israel.* Cardiff: University of Wales Press, 1955.

MOWINCKEL, SIGMUND. *He that Cometh.* Translated by G. W. Anderson. New York and Nashville: Abingdon, 1954.

HOOKE, S. H. (ed.). *Myth, Ritual, and Kingship.* New York: Oxford University Press, 1958.

The Psalms

BENTZEN, AAGE. *King and Messiah.* London: Lutterworth, 1955.

SZIKSZAI, S. "King," in *The Interpreter's Dictionary of the Bible.* Vol. 3, pp. 15 f.

EISSFELDT, O. *The Old Testament: An Introduction.* Pp. 102-04 ("kingship") and pp. 109-111, especially the literature cited in note 23 on p. 109 and also on p. 737 ("enthronement" or "accession").

HUMMEL, H. D. "Survey of Recent Literature," in Herbert F. Hahn, *The Old Testament in Modern Research.* Expanded ed. Philadelphia: Fortress Press, 1966. Pp. 277-80 and 280-82.

NOTH, MARTIN. "God, King, Nation in the Old Testament," in *The Laws in the Pentateuch and Other Studies,* trans. D. R. Ap-Thomas. Philadelphia: Fortress Press, 1967, Pp. 145-78.

SNAITH, N. H. *The Jewish New Year Festival.* London: SPCK, 1947. Criticism of Mowinckel's views, pp. 195-200.

McCULLOUGH, W. S. "The 'Enthronement of Yahweh' Psalms," in *A Stubborn Faith: Papers on Old Testament and Related Subjects Presented to Honor William Andrew Irwin.* Edited by E. C. Hobbs. Dallas: Southern Methodist University Press, 1956. Pp. 53-61.

DE VAUX, ROLAND, O. P. *Ancient Israel: Its Life and Institutions.* Translated by John McHugh. New York: McGraw-Hill, 1961. See especially pp. 100-114 on the king (coronation, enthronement psalms, the king, and worship) and pp. 504-06 on "enthronement psalms."

LIPIŃSKI, E. *La royauté de Yahwé dans la poésie et le culte de l'áncien Israel.* Brussels: Koninklijke Academie, 1965. Psalms 47, 93, 96–99.

ON THE "I" OF THE PSALMS

ROBINSON, H. WHEELER. *Corporate Personality in Ancient Israel.* ("Facet Books—Biblical Series," 11.) Philadelphia: Fortress Press, 1964. Pp. 12-14, with further references there and on pp. 38-39.

EISSFELDT, O. *The Old Testament: An Introduction.* P. 115.

RINGGREN, HELMER. *The Faith of Qumran.* Pp. 15 f.

BARDTKE, H. "Das Ich des Meisters in den *Hodajoth* von Qumrân," *Wissenschaftliche Zeitschrift der Karl-Marx-Universität Leipzig,* 6 (1956/57), pp. 93-104.

DUPONT-SUMMER, A. *The Essene Writings from Qumran.* Translated by G. Vermes. ("Meridian Books.") Cleveland and New York: World Publishing Company, 1961. Pp. 199-201.

On Psalm Poetry

GRAY, GEORGE BUCHANAN. *The Forms of Hebrew Poetry considered with Special Reference to the Criticism and Interpretation of the Old Testament.* London: Hodder & Stoughton, 1915. Reprinted, with a prolegomenon by David N. Freedman (New York: Ktav Publishing House, 1967).

GEVIRTZ, STANLEY. *Patterns in the Early Poetry of Israel.* ("Studies in Ancient Oriental Civilization," 32.) Chicago: University of Chicago Press, 1963.

(See also under "Commentaries and Treatments for the General Reader.")

On Individual Psalms, Groups of Psalms, and Special Aspects

Ps. 8   CHILDS, BREVARD S. "Psalm 8 in the Context of the Christian Canon," *Interpretation,* 23 (1969), pp. 20–31.

Pss. 9-10   GORDIS, ROBERT. "Psalms 9-10—A Textual and Exegetical Study," *Jewish Quarterly Review,* 48 (1957), pp. 104-12.

Ps. 51   DALGLISH, EDWARD R. *Psalm Fifty-One in the Light of Ancient Near Eastern Patternism.* Leiden: Brill, 1962.

Ps. 89   AHLSTRÖM, G. W. *Psalm 89, Eine Liturgie aus dem Ritual des leidenden Königs.* Lund: Gleerups, 1959.

Ps. 92   SARNA, NAHUM A. "The Psalm for the Sabbath Day (Ps 92)," *Journal of Biblical Literature,* 81 (1962), pp. 155-68.

Ps. 110   DÜRR, LORENZ. *Psalm 110 im Lichte der neueren alttestamentlichen Forschung.* Münster: Aschendorff, 1929.

Ps. 132   FRETHEIM, TERENCE E. "Psalm 132: A Form-Critical Study," *Journal of Biblical Literature,* 86 (1967), pp. 289–300.

Ps. 139   HOLMAN, JAN. "The Structure of Psalm CXXXIX," *Vetus Testamentum,* 21 (1971), pp. 298–310.

BIRKELAND, HARRIS. *The Evildoers in the Psalms.* Oslo: Dybwad, 1955.

BUSS, MARTIN J. "The Psalms of Asaph and Korah," *Journal of Biblical Literature,* 82 (1963), pp. 382-92.

CRIM, KEITH R. *The Royal Psalms.* Richmond: John Knox Press, 1962.

DELEKAT, L. *Asylie und Schutzorakel am Zionheiligtum: Eine Untersuchung zu den Privaten Feindpsalmen.* Leiden: Brill, 1967.

FROST, S. B. "Asservation by Thanksgiving," *Vetus Testamentum,* 8 (1958), pp. 380-90.

MOWINCKEL, SIGMUND. "Notes on the Psalms," *Studia Theologica,* 13 (1959), pp. 134-56.

SCHMIDT, HANS. *Das Gebet der Angeklagten in den Psalmen.* ("Beihefte zur Zeitschrift für die alttestamentliche Wissenschaft," 46.) Giessen: Töpelmann, 1928.

SNAITH, N. H. *Hymns of the Temple.* London: SCM, 1951.

Studies on Psalms. ("Oudtestamentische Studien," 13.) Edited by P. A. H. de Boer. Leiden: Brill, 1963. Includes "The Psalms: style-figures and structure," by N. H. Ridderbos.

TERRIEN, SAMUEL. "Creation, Cultus, and Faith in the Psalter," in *Horizons of Theological Education: Essays in Honor of Charles L. Taylor.* Edited by J. B. Coburn, W. D. Wagoner, and J. H. Ziegler. Dayton: American Association of Theological Seminaries, 1966. Pp. 116–28.

TSEVAT, M. *A Study of the Language of the Biblical Psalms.* ("Journal of Biblical Literature Monograph Series," 9.) Philadelphia: Society of Biblical Literature, 1955.

WEVERS, J. W. "A Study in the Form Criticism of Individual Complaint Psalms," *Vetus Testamentum,* 6 (1956), pp. 80-96.